THE SURVIVAL GUIDE FOR BUSINESS FAMILIES

THE SURVIVAL GUIDE
FOR BUSINESS FAMILIES

Gerald Le Van

Routledge
New York London

Published in 1999 by
Routledge
29 West 35th Street
New York, NY 10001

Published in Great Britain by
Routledge
11 New Fetter Lane
London EC4P 4EE

Copyright © 1999 by Routledge

Printed in the United States of America on acid-free paper.
Interior Design by: Mary Neal Meador

All rights reserved. No part of this book may be reprinted or reproduced or utilized in
any form or by any electronic, mechanical, or other means, now known or hereafter
invented, including photocopying and recording or in any information storage or
retrieval system, without permission in writing from the publishers.

Library of Congress Cataloging-in-Publication Data

Le Van, Gerald.
    The survival guide for business families / Gerald Le Van.
        p.   cm.
    Includes bibliographical references (p. 201) and index.
    ISBN 0-415-92086-8
    1. Family-owned business enterprises—Management.   2. Family-owned
business enterprises—Succession.   I. Title.
HD62.25.L48   1998
658'.045—DC21   98-7429
                                                                        CIP

CONTENTS

With deepest appreciation . . .

- To our client business families who have hired us to help them grow through their troubles, and who are still growing.

- To my ancestors, the Le Vans, the Guinns, the Bells, and the Hintons for all their gifts that survive, but have been lost to memory.

- To my parents, Nolan Guinn Le Van and Mary Bell Le Van, who bore me, raised me, challenged me, and loved me.

- To my wife, Sara, whose understanding of families could fill several books, and whose nurturing grace continues to astonish me after more than forty years.

- To our children, Liz, Guy, and Marthe, who continue to teach us the most profound lessons about being a family. May parenting never end.

- To my mentors in the law, Stuart D. Lunn and the late Judge Alvin B. Rubin, and to my psychological mentor, colleague, neighbor, and friend, David E. Lange, Ph.D.

- To Nancy A. Walker for her devotion and loyalty, to Margaret Marchuk for her patience and editorial skills, and to Melissa A. Rosati, my editor at Routledge, for her energy, encouragement, and good humor.

Gerald Le Van
April 1998

PREFACE

By 1986, I had been a Louisiana lawyer for twenty-five years.

Almost half of that time had been spent teaching law school courses on trusts and estates. Estate planning was my favorite area of the law. I had written a book about Louisiana wills and trusts, made lots of speeches about estate planning, and considered myself to be a mature and competent trust and estates lawyer. Then my life changed forever.

In 1986, two of my largest clients—both heads of large and successful, family-owned businesses—came to see me with similar problems. There was conflict in each family about the future role of the younger generation in the business. In typical lawyer fashion, I set out to "fix" both families—only to realize I had two serious concerns to address.

My first concern was ethical: Who *really* was my client? Was my client the business leader? His unhappy children? Their company? Was I facing a serious conflict of interest by trying to be a lawyer to all of them?

My second concern was more serious: I really did not understand family dynamics. Years of law had not prepared me to help guide these families through their rocky relationships, their difficult communications, their emotional agenda, their rivalries, their differing versions of reality.

When a respected friend suggested that a psychologist be

brought in to help these families, I resisted. Wouldn't the mere suggestion of a psychologist to these families also suggest that they were "sick" or "crazy"? And wouldn't that get me fired as their lawyer? My friend persisted, and, with some resistance, each family accepted that suggestion.

What happened amazed me. The psychologist seemed to understand the dynamics of the family relationships. He got them to open up, to air their understandings and misunderstandings, to improve and to manage their business communications. Eventually, each family worked out the future role of its younger generation in the business.

The following year, David Lange, a local psychologist, referred a wealthy couple to me for estate planning. David had been working with them in marital therapy. After interviewing the couple extensively, I presented them with what I thought to be an elegant estate plan. The husband refused to sign the documents. Taking this as a sign he needed further therapy, I tendered the couple back to David, who suggested he and I see the couple together in a joint session. Had I not had the experience with my own business family clients, I would have thought David's suggestion to be, well, crazy. But we both met with the troubled couple, and they subsequently completed their estate planning.

In 1990, I left law practice for North Carolina and full-time family business consulting. In 1994, David Lange closed his therapy practice and joined me as chief psychologist in the consulting practice.

This book is my version of our combined consulting experience with business families. Although recognized as family business consultants, our work is much broader: We prefer to think and talk of *business families*. In common parlance, "family business" connotes an operating company. For us, "business family" refers to two or more relatives who own family-generated wealth, which may be an operating company. An operating company may be only a minor part, however, or there may be no operating company. A business family may own real estate together, or be partners in a family limited partnership that holds investments. They may be the heirs of an estate or beneficiaries of a trust: The descendants of Henry Ford are a business family, although Ford Motor Company is publicly held; as trust beneficiaries, John D. Rockefeller's heirs are nevertheless a business family—as are the JacMars, who are presented in this book, and who are struggling over the future of JacMar Corporation.

Business families play a huge role in the global economy. In the United States, they generate more than 50 percent of the gross domestic product, and some 160 of the Fortune 500 companies are family controlled—familiar names like Marriott, Wal-Mart, Estee Lauder, and Gerber. Business families also dominate the economies of Western Europe, South America, and the Pacific Rim, where public ownership of large companies is much less common. Yet the prominence of business families went largely unnoticed until the 1980s, when post–World War II entrepreneurs began to approach retirement age. They found themselves facing agonizing questions about the future:

- Shall I keep the business or sell it?

- If we keep the business in the family, who should succeed me as CEO?

- If we keep the business, who should own it after me?

- If we keep the business, how do we reconcile the interests of family members who work for the company, and those who pursue other interests?

Family dynamics play a powerful and often overriding role in business relationships. This is why I use the word "family" as the noun. "Business family" focuses primary attention where it belongs—on the family.

A family is an emotional institution. Business families are a glorious, curious, and often maddening mix of family ways and business necessities. The levels of trust and loyalty within the family affect how they run the business as well. A strong family business is the most formidable competitor in the marketplace—not because family members are smarter or work harder than anyone else (although often they do), but because family members weave an intangible emotional network and values. This family solidarity can give the business the strength it needs to draw from during rough times in the marketplace.

The JacMar family in this book is entirely hypothetical. They represent a composite of first-generation, entrepreneurial client families we have helped over the years. Their business is successful and stable, the company mature. The sons entered the business without clear career plans, and Jack, the founder, is approaching retirement age with no plan other than to work as long as he can, or at least until his sons show more promise as business leaders. Jack is wealthy, but most of his wealth is locked up in JacMar Corporation, so his future financial security hinges upon the company's continued success. Tensions about the future of the younger generation in the business have not surfaced yet—but it's just a matter of time.

This self-help book is designed to help business families identify the *work* they must do to secure their future. At the outset, I ask 39 Critical Questions that each business family should consider seriously in defining its work. Then, chapter by chapter, the JacMar family struggles to answer these questions. The JacMars' answers to all 39 Critical Questions—hammered out over the intervening chapters—appear in the final chapter as their *interim* agenda for the future.

As consultants, we are frequently retained by business families who are "stuck." They are stuck because they can't seem to ask these 39 Critical Questions, can't recognize their importance or urgency. They are families who can't agree on their answers, or who haven't found ways to discuss the questions productively and without conflict. When "stuck" families answer the 39 Critical Questions, they always discover answers that help them define their work.

We also asked stuck families to read this book. Many of them identify with the JacMars and are relieved to find out they are not alone in facing critical issues. Perhaps you will recognize your clients—or yourselves.

Gerald Le Van
Black Mountain, North Carolina
January 1998

INTRODUCTION

FOR BUSINESS FAMILIES

Your business family has work to do! For the sake of your family and the wealth your family has created, your family's work must be done. If your *family work* is not done well:

- You could lose your business.

- Your wealth could decline or disappear.

- You could fall into treacherous family lawsuits.

- Your family relationships could be irreparably damaged.

Your family work can only be done by family members. Others outside the family—your lawyer, your accountant, your financial advisor—have important parts to play, but they cannot do their jobs unless (and perhaps until) your family work is completed. There are no quick, easy, cheap substitutes for family work; it takes time, patience, and dedication. *Beware of outsiders who promise your family pat answers*. They do not work.

This book is designed to help identify your family work by asking the members of your family to answer the 39 Critical Questions, from which your family will discover those factors that are critical to the future of your business family. Your family work is to arrive at a collective answer to those questions. Remember, no one else can answer them for you.

It is always a comfort for business families to discover that they are not alone—that other business families confront some of the same perplexing issues. So let me introduce the JacMar family—a first-generation, entrepreneurial family whose story unfolds as they wrestle with issues raised by the 39 Critical Questions:

- Is the younger generation really ready to lead?

- Can the older generation safely let go?

- Are the children really committed to make the company grow?

- What should be the rules for family members employed by the company?

- What is their fair compensation? How should their job performance be evaluated?

- Who should own stock, and how should stock ownership be transferred?

- How can inside and outside family shareholders be reconciled?

Because the 39 Critical Questions can raise sensitive issues, some families avoid them, deny their importance, pretend they are not relevant. Yet the most efficient and effective way to do your family work is to address the Critical Questions *as a group.* This means you must meet, talk, and decide together. Some families fear the risk in this: someone might get upset—cry, yell; someone might stay away or storm out of the meeting room; just talking about these sensitive issues might damage relationships, hurt feelings, alienate the family. That is possible, of course. The worst damage, however, is likely to come from *not* talking; from *not* trying!

Lots of good things can (and will) happen as your business family answers the 39 Critical Questions together:

- Your future together will become clearer, more manageable, less threatening.

- Old misunderstandings will be put aside; traditional assumptions and positions will be re-examined, clarified, perhaps even changed.

- Every family member will get a voice, a hearing, a respectful audience.

- Your family will learn how to deliberate and decide issues together.

- You will develop a process for making important decisions in the future.

- Each family member will "buy in" to your new process of discussing and deciding.

- Each family member will "own" your family's answers to the 39 Critical Questions, because he or she helped create those answers.

- Each family member should perceive himself or herself as a winner in a win-win situation.

- Your family will become its stronger, better self. It will be transformed.

The 39 Critical Questions are found later in this Introduction; they are addressed in detail in chapters within the book.

FOR OUTSIDE ADVISORS TO BUSINESS FAMILIES

Sim City is a popular computer game with young Americans, in which the player is challenged to design and build a virtual city. All sorts of problems are presented: layouts of streets; utilities; transportation; zoning of residential, commercial, and industrial areas; city planning; sanitation; police and fire protection. Just point and click. Need a zoning variance? No public hearing is required, no angry neighbors pour out their discontents before political appointees. Just point and click.

A business family is not a computer game. Yet sometimes outside advisors treat them like characters in a virtual drama. Just

point and click. Advisors press families to reorganize their operations, plan their estates, reorder their business and personal
finances—before family members can even *hear* them. Such
business families, for all sorts of reasons, haven't yet found a way
to talk and decide about important business issues that must be
addressed in the interest of their future security. These families
are "stuck."

The most powerful obstacles to constructive business talk in
stuck families are the "soft" ones: emotional, relational, and
familial issues. Soft obstacles are the most frustrating to well-
intentioned advisors, who are expert in the "hard" disciplines:
organizational development, business and estate planning, tax
avoidance and deferral, financial strategies. But if the family is
really stuck, it's difficult for them to concentrate on or even hear
about the hard issues—about buy-sell agreements, recapitaliza-
tion, strategic planning, wills, trusts, life insurance. Pushing the
hard advice confuses a stuck family, and may slow down the
process of unsticking themselves.

Why is this? Because a business family is an *emotional institution.* To be helpful and effective, outside advisors must honor the
family's emotional agenda. I hear advisors refer to this "soft"
area as "touchy-feely," but in my view, the phrase "touchy-feely"
dishonors the interwoven agenda that business families must
address. A stuck family hasn't intentionally erected emotional
barriers to hard products and services, it simply isn't ready yet to
hear about them. Before the business family can give you its
undivided attention, it must do its family work.

As a trusted outside advisor, there are some things you can do
to help a client family who undertakes family work:

- See that this book is made available to each family member.

- Remember to include spouses, who may play a powerful
  role. Don't forget younger family members and teenagers.

- Some family members aren't readers. You may need to
  introduce them to the 39 Critical Questions and the JacMar

family by talking about them. Read important parts to them, or perhaps make an audiotape version.

- Encourage family members to discuss among themselves the issues raised in this book, but don't attempt to lead a family group discussion unless you are trained in family dynamics.

- Scrutinize each family member's answers to the 39 Critical Questions.

- Once the family selects which of the 39 Critical Questions define their family work, encourage them to write down their issues and objectives.

- Suggest a schedule of regular meetings to address their family work. They may ask you to be present, but don't feel neglected if they don't. You aren't part of the family and may not belong in those meetings. If you are invited, you may want to decline unless you are trained in family dynamics.

- Don't be too eager for a quick solution. Most constructive change in families takes time—it may be eighteen months or more.

- If the family isn't making progress, or abandons the process, and appears to remain stuck, consider recommending professional family business consultants.

If your clients are able to do their family work by themselves but need a "jump start," this book will help them begin. Your encouragement will help them keep working until they are finished.

A final note: Included in the Appendices are materials addressed especially to you. They should be quite helpful as your client family does its work.

THE 39 CRITICAL QUESTIONS

Read each question carefully. Determine how important each question is to the survival of your family business.

If the answer to that question is *critical* to the future of your family business—if your family must answer that question to get on with its future—write a "2" in the space to the left of the question.

If the answer to the question is not critical, but still *important* to the future of your business, write a "1" in the space to the left.

If the answer to the question is *irrelevant*—or if your family has already answered that question—put a "0" in the space to the left.

1. ___ Are we committed to the future of our family business?

2. ___ Are we obligated to work there indefinitely, or may we pursue other careers?

3. ___ Do we want to own the business or should it be sold?

4. ___ How do we decide which family members will be employed by the company?

5. ___ Must we offer every family member a job?

6. ___ Should in-laws or other relatives be invited to work in the business?

7. ___ What education or work preparation should be required of family members who work in the business?

8. ___ How do we assign titles and work responsibility?

9. ___ How should we evaluate and pay family members who work in the business?

10. ___ What should we do if a family member doesn't perform or leaves the business?

11. ___ How do we select the next leader of the company?

12. ___ When do we decide who will be the next leader of the company?

13. ___ When and how should leadership transition take place?

14. ___ How do we evaluate our new leader's job performance?

15. ___ How do we provide meaningful careers for other family members who are not chosen to lead?

16. ___ Who should serve on our board of directors? Family members? Employees? Our outside advisors? Others?

17. ___ How should our board of directors function?

18. ___ What should we expect of our directors?

19. ___ Who should own stock in the business?

20. ___ Should all children own equally, whether or not they work in the business?

21. ___ What dividends or perquisites (perks) should shareholders receive?

22. ___ How do we balance the interests of inside family shareholders (who work in the business) with the interests of outside family shareholders (who don't work in the business)?

23. ___ What do we do if a family shareholder wants to sell out?

24. ___ How should we deal with family disagreements? (Between

individuals? Between members of the same or different generations?)

25. ___ How do we teach in-laws and younger family members about the values and traditions of our business and our family?

26. ___ Who will lead family activities in the next generation?

27. ___ How do we help family members who are in financial distress?

28. ___ What other responsibilities do we have to other family members?

29. ___ What do we do if there is a divorce in the family?

30. ___ What if a family member breaks the law or is seriously irresponsible?

31. ___ How do we support family members in their own business ventures?

32. ___ How do we protect the contributions of unrelated, key employees?

33. ___ To what extent do we involve key employees in family disagreements?

34. ___ What obligations do we have to prized employees?

35. ___ Should key employees own stock in our family business?

36. ___ Might one key employee be the next leader of our business?

37. ___ How do we treat loyal employees whose productivity or value to the company has declined?

38. ___ What are our responsibilities to the community?

39. ___ How do we cope with our public image and the public's expectations of us?

Now, total the numbers you have inserted on each page.

Enter your total here: _____

Are there other questions your business family needs to answer? If so, please write those questions in the following spaces and assign a "2" for critical, a "1" for important, or a "0" for irrelevant or already answered to the left of each question, just as you did above.

Additional questions for our family business:

_____

_____

_____

_____

_____

_____

_____

Now that you have weighed the importance of each question, compare your responses with other family members and see if you want to change some of your responses. You may want to *raise* the number in some instances because the question is more important than you thought at first.

If there is to be a family discussion of the 39 Critical Questions, make a chart that reflects everyone's response (see Figure 1). If a question draws a "2" from most family members, it likely spots a sensitive issue. Be sure to include the total scores at the bottom for each family member. If the score of a family member is around 40 or more, chances are he or she senses a number of unresolved issues. If a score is around 10 or less, the family member is likely distant from the situation or for some reason is not focused on the critical issues.

Be especially attentive to Question 24, that deals with family disagreements. If most family members rate Question 24 as a "2," then family discussions about the 39 Critical Questions could be quite sensitive. Your family might want to consider an expert outside discussion leader for those sessions.

Figure 1
Summarizing Critical Responses

Question #1	Jack	Margaret	JJ	Frank	Karen
1					
2					
3					
4					
5					
6					
7					
8					
9					
10					
11					
12					
13					
14					
15					
16					
17					
18					
19					
20					
21					
22					
23					
24					
25					
26					
27					
28					
29					
30					
31					
32					
33					
34					
35					
36					
37					
38					
39					

Part One

THE JACMAR BUSINESS FAMILY

1

INTRODUCING THE JACMARS

Like most teenagers if my parents had said, "This is what you are going to do," I would have replied, "No it is not."
—*John W. Marriott III, General Manager, Marriott Corporation*[1]

As his troop ship neared San Francisco, Jack made himself three promises:

- He would become an engineer.

- He would marry Margaret as soon as possible.

- He would never again take orders from incompetent persons like he had met in the Army.

Jack had been drafted into the Army in 1953, near the end of the Korean War. Assigned to a construction battalion, it became clear that Jack could fix almost anything—with or without the official spare parts.

The oldest of four children, Jack had little time for sports, dates, or other extracurricular activities. Jack worked all he could, contributed his earnings to the family, and helped care for his younger brother and sisters. Jack's father worked only intermittently, his mother worked at home, sometimes taking in laundry and ironing.

After his discharge from the Army, Jack married Margaret and entered college, financed by the G.I. Bill of Rights. Their first son, Jack Jr., "JJ," was born during Jack's midterm examinations the following year. At one point Jack held three part-time jobs to help support his family. By the time Jack graduated with honors in mechanical engineering, he was the proud father of his second son, Frank.

Jack landed his first job as a junior engineer with a large engineering consulting firm whose principal clients were military suppliers. Almost immediately, he knew he had made a mistake. In Jack's view, his employer was trying to help civilian incompetents deal with military incompetents. Jack was miserable. He would submit his work but seldom see it again, he got little feedback, his supervisor was incompetent, and Jack argued with him frequently. After a particularly violent quarrel, Jack was fired.

Almost thirty years old, with a wife, two small boys, and little savings, Jack was unemployed. But he was determined to show them. Fascinated with several unsolved engineering problems at his former firm, Jack began tinkering with them, first in his garage, then in a rented warehouse. He developed some solutions, patented the processes, formed JacMar Corporation, and went into business.

JACK THE ENTREPRENEUR

Jack's work style is fairly typical of successful entrepreneurs. Until recently, Jack always enjoyed good health and blinding energy—gifts that are almost universal among entrepreneurs. For most of his life, Jack has worked sixty to seventy hours per week. He lacks respect for others who don't work hard and long. His sons have much more relaxed work styles, and this causes problems.

Jack is brilliant but also highly intuitive. He listens to his gut, to his instincts. Sometimes he struggles to explain why he made a particular business decision, but Jack is not a good teacher; to him, the lessons are obvious. He lacks patience with those who don't understand him the first time he speaks. This too causes problems with his sons.

Although there is no stereotypical "entrepreneurial personality," biographies of famous entrepreneurs like Henry Ford or An Wang reveal striking parallels in their personalities, work styles, successes, and shortcomings.

THE JACMAR ORGANIZATION

Organizationally, JacMar Corporation is fairly primitive—in some respects, downright sloppy. Although Jack inspires his people, he is poor at delegation. Jack is very "hands on," very controlling, watching everything and everyone. A functional organization chart would look like a spider web with Jack in the middle, reacting to every vibration. There is little depth of management in the company except for Al, the general manager who took over during Jack's heart surgery three years ago, and Jack's sons JJ and Frank.

What JacMar Corporation lacks in organization, it more than makes up for in talent. Jack's stable of gifted technical people is the envy of his competitors. Gifted people challenged by a gifted leader—this is the success story of JacMar Corporation

Inside Your Business Family . . .

Who was the founder of your family business? What were the circumstances of its founding? Was there a single precipitating event? Is there a file or scrapbook containing the founding documents, such as your original corporate charter, newspaper stories, photographs? Do your family members know the story of how your business was founded? Do your key employees know the story?

If you were going to produce a videotape about the founding of your business, what would you want the viewers to see? Who would you want to see your videotape?

2

JACMAR'S BUSINESS PROFILE

Lillian and Fred complement each other perfectly—one is a classic entrepreneur, the other a professional manager.
—Gordon Muckler, Vice President of Marketing,
Lillian Vernon Corporation [2]

Most entrepreneurial enterprises go through four definable stages (see Figure 2).

Stage One: Start-up. The first five years or so are the "start-up" years. Nearly 80 percent of all businesses fail during the start-up phase, many because of inadequate capitalization (in other words, they run out of money). Like many other entrepreneurial founders, the start-up phase for Jack involved years of ceaseless work, risk, connivance, and ingenuity. Jack learned how to survive. During those tough early years, Jack teetered several times on the brink of bankruptcy and almost lost the business. But he persevered, and he succeeded. It was Jack's financial savvy that made the difference.

During those early years Margaret worked in the business, doing jobs that Jack didn't have time for or couldn't afford to hire someone to do. She was never paid for her services to JacMar Corporation, and she still resents that. Near the end of the fran-

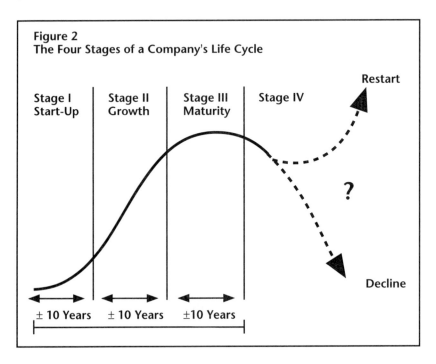

Figure 2
The Four Stages of a Company's Life Cycle

tic first phase, their daughter, Karen, was born. Margaret quit working for JacMar Corporation. With Jack's long hours and frequent travel, Margaret felt she needed to be at home to hold the family together.

Stage Two: Growth. The next ten years or so—Stage Two—are exhilarating. The business has taken hold, and sales and profits are taking off. During the growth phase, JacMar Corporation blossomed because its patented processes were much in demand, and because of Jack's uncanny ability to attract and motivate gifted technical employees. Jack was demanding and exacting, driving his people to solve customers' problems "on time and under bid." JacMar's 200 employees are fiercely loyal, and each feels personally attached to Jack. They both love and fear him. Jack has the "charismatic" personality of a born leader.

Employees have always known where they stood with Jack, although it might be uncomfortable. Jack was always looking for fresh approaches, new options, and his creativity excited his employees to discover new and better ways of doing things. A restless visionary, Jack was always changing things. The work environment was chaotic, but always exciting. In spite of past accomplishments, Jack's restless imagination drove others to do better. During its phenomenal growth stage, JacMar Corporation was featured in *Inc. Magazine.*

Stage Three: Maturity. After about twenty years or so, a successful entrepreneurial business matures. Growth slows down, market share and profits stay relatively flat; depreciation overtakes research and development, and the family takes more out of the business. Over the last five years, JacMar's gross sales have increased from $24.6 million to $30 million, an average of 5 percent per year. Earnings before interest, taxes, depreciation, and amortization (EBITDA) grew from $2.5 million five years ago to $3.4 million two years ago, but dipped to $2.1 million last year because of outside factors (mostly due to a recession). The EBITDA calculation allows investors to compare the "earnings stream" of a company to the earnings stream of other investments. The value of a company can be stated as a multiple, e.g., six times EBITDA. The reciprocal fraction (EBITDA divided by six) is the rough equivalent of a price/earnings ratio used to value publicly held companies.

The life cycle of an entrepreneurial company often parallels the life cycle of its founder. This may be happening at JacMar Corporation. Margaret has noticed some changes in Jack since his heart surgery three years ago. He is less communicative and seems preoccupied. They have vacationed in Florida for the past several years, last year for more than a month. At times Jack seemed to enjoy Florida, but he became restless, calling the office several times a day. Margaret helped him reduce his calls to a few per week. At the office, however, no one wanted to make decisions without Jack's approval, since he has a way of reversing whatever others decide in his absence.

Jack never took the time to develop hobbies, although he had some golf lessons and went fishing with friends several times. As a result, his vacation time with Margaret weighed heavily on both of them. It's pretty clear neither wants Jack to retire and come home. For Jack, work is life, and he is afraid of retirement: too many of his friends have died after they quit work. Not to work would seem like suicide—yet Jack is slowing down; nature is taking care of that. The life cycle of JacMar Corporation is following Jack's own life cycle.

During the first ten years, Jack was all vigor and ingenuity; his company survived. During the second ten years, Jack was all vision and genius, and JacMar Corporation became a major player. Now, during its third decade, Jack seems to have lost his edge, his daring, his drive for "we can do better." Jack senses this crisis, and it worries him greatly. Margaret has picked up the signal, and JJ is worried also. Will there be enough left of JacMar Corporation to prosper in his generation?

Stage Four: Restart or decline. A business can remain "mature" only for a limited time. It will decline unless restarted. The mature JacMar company reflects Jack's aging. Although the company made its reputation on the cutting edge of technical expertise, research and development are declining. Sales are flat, and JacMar's market share is not growing. The family is taking more out of the company, so depreciation is overtaking investment.

Today, Jack and Margaret are in a "savoring mode," enjoying the recognition that comes with entrepreneurial success. They are pleased with their reputation in their local community and are proud of the company logo on the water tower, on their trucks, in trade magazines. Jack is a long-time director of their principal bank, although JacMar Corporation has no long-term bank debt. Jack served many years on the board of their industry trade association, including two terms as chairman. However, he and Margaret no longer look forward to the annual conventions.

The JacMars read "horror stories" in the business press about destructive lawsuits among warring business families. They hear about the distressing failure rate of family businesses—a widespread but discredited statistic that only one in three family-owned businesses survives successfully in the second generation.

THE ISSUE FACING JACMAR

Mature companies like JacMar Corporation dare not rest on past accomplishments. Either JacMar Corporation reorganizes and restarts, or it begins to sink rapidly. Jack has built a marvelous launch pad for the next generation, but if the launch isn't made soon, JacMar Corporation will ultimately go out of business. Jack senses this dilemma, that his company needs a reorganizational jump start, but he lacks the motivation to lead it. To guide JacMar Corporation safely through its fourth phase will require different leadership that he cannot provide. Margaret insists that one of their sons can provide that leadership . . . eventually.

But not right now.

Inside Your Business Family . . .

Which of the typical stages describes your family business? Stage Two? Stage Three? Stage Four? Review your annual earnings for the past five years.

Calculate your EBITDA—earnings before interest and taxes. Project your EBITDA over the next three years.

How is your company owned? In the margin, list the numbers of shares outstanding in each class of stock, the names of each shareholder, the number and percentage of shares in each class owned by each shareholder. Are you a Subchapter S corporation?

How does Jack's leadership style compare with the style of your business leader? How do the age and health of your business leader affect your company? How does he or she face retirement?

3

THE FAMILY DIMENSION

When your [family's] name is on the door, you take what you do
very personally.

—Robert D. Haas, CEO, Levi Strauss & Co.[3]

A family business is no different from any other business—
except in one very important respect: The company is family
owned or family controlled. More often than not, family members hold key management positions in the company. This
family dimension—powerful, sometimes subtle, sometimes un-
detected—sets these enterprises apart from all others. So let's
examine some basic understandings about families.

A diagram of a "family tree" is often used by outside advisors
such as lawyers, accountants and financial advisors. Their principal concern is ownership and family property—with "who gets
what from whom?" The diagram of the JacMar family in Figure 3
is typical.

A family tree diagram doesn't undertake to diagram family
relationships. Yet family relationships are the sources of both
power and trouble in business families. Psychologists have a way
of diagraming family relationships known as a "genogram."
Later on you will see a genogram of the JacMar family. However,

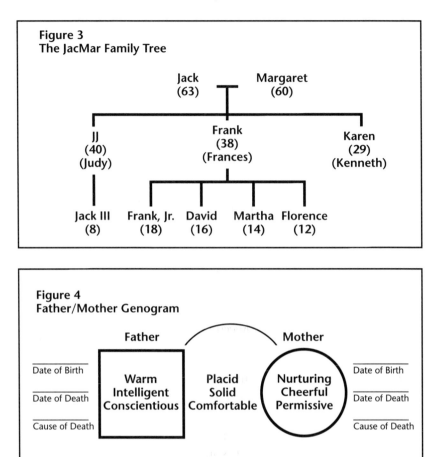

Figure 3
The JacMar Family Tree

Figure 4
Father/Mother Genogram

to really appreciate how a genogram diagrams relationships, you should draw a genogram of your own family. This is how to begin.

GENOGRAM

A genogram assumes that men are square and women are round. Draw a box for each male; a circle for each female. Begin your own genogram with a box representing your father, and a circle representing your mother (see Figure 4). Near the box representing your father, write his date of birth and date of death

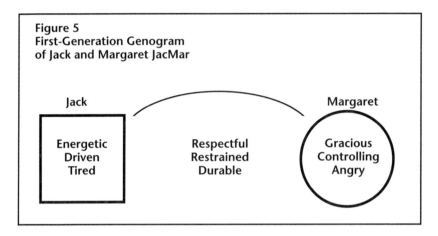

Figure 5
First-Generation Genogram
of Jack and Margaret JacMar

Jack   Margaret

Energetic	Respectful	Gracious
Driven	Restrained	Controlling
Tired	Durable	Angry

and cause of death, if deceased. Next write three words inside the square that best describe him. For example, you might describe your father as distant or warm; firm or indulgent; conscientious or irresponsible. Take your time before you write. Repeat this exercise for your mother near the circle, taking your time before writing down her qualities.

Draw a straight line between your father (box) and mother (circle), representing their marriage. If they divorced, draw a slash through that line and write the year of their divorce.

Next, draw a *curved line* between your father (box) and mother (circle) representing their relationship. Write three words near that curved line that best describe their relationship. For example, you might describe their relationship as placid or stormy; solid or shaky; comfortable or edgy. Now you have a beginning genogram of your parents' generation (see Jack and Margaret's in Figure 5).

Now, below the diagram of your parents, draw boxes and circles representing your generation—yourself and your siblings. Begin with the oldest sibling on the left, and proceed from left to right by birth order, showing your youngest sibling on the right. Figure 6 shows the second generation of the JacMar family.

Identify yourself in the second generation of your genogram.

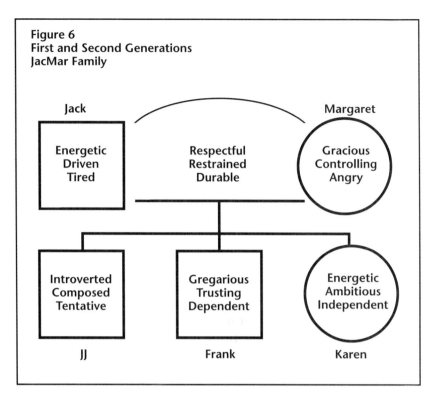

Figure 6
First and Second Generations
JacMar Family

Jack

Energetic
Driven
Tired

Respectful
Restrained
Durable

Margaret

Gracious
Controlling
Angry

Introverted
Composed
Tentative

Gregarious
Trusting
Dependent

Energetic
Ambitious
Independent

JJ   Frank   Karen

Inside the box or circle identifying you, write three words that best describe *you*. For instance you may describe yourself as aggressive or passive, thoughtful or impulsive, quiet or boisterous.

BIRTH ORDER

Every time a child is born, a new family is created. The old family no longer exists. Birth order has a great deal to do with who we are and where we fit in our families. You are either an oldest, middle, youngest, or an only child.

Alfred Adler, the pioneer psychologist, was one of the first to see the connection. He discovered that birth order has much to do with our behavior, our development, our outlook. Interest in birth order has prompted continuing research, yet there is much more to be learned. Even so, what is already known about birth order offers fascinating insights into family dynamics. And birth order is always critical to business families.

Oldest children tend to be very conscientious and reliable. They usually have higher IQs, make better grades, and go to school longer than their siblings. Tense, competitive, even driven, Oldests are more career oriented, stubborn, even compulsive. Look for migraine headaches in Oldests.

Middle children tend to be peacemakers and people persons. They make friends, are very sociable, make good negotiators. Middlers like to avoid confrontation and may feel inferior and closed in when under pressure. Good at keeping secrets, the Middler personality is the darling of corporate America.

Youngest children tend to be artistic, funny, affectionate, caring, fun loving, disorganized. You want Youngests at your parties. Watch for their "Who's going to take care of me?" attitude—someone *did* take care of them during their younger years. They may have felt pressure to remain the "baby" of the family.

Only children often turn out like super Oldests. Extremely reliable and conscientious, they may be super conservative because they were raised by adults and spent much time around their parents.

If there is an age gap of five or more years between two children, you can almost draw a line and start another family. The first child born on the younger side of that gap will probably have Oldest characteristics. In large families, there may be more than one Oldest, for example, the first-born boy, the first-born girl, and perhaps the first born after a five-year gap.

In the second generation JacMars, JJ seems to fit the Oldest pattern. Frank comes out of the Middler mold. Born seven years after Frank, Karen may be the "second" Oldest in this family. Perhaps her birth order helps explain Karen's career orientation, her independence, and her conflicts with her brother JJ

Now let's consider some interesting speculation about marriage and birth order.

- If both spouses are Oldests, this could mean two strong-willed people continually butting heads from day one or, in order to get along, two realistic people creating a controller-pleaser situation.

- If husband and wife are both Middlers, their marriage could be suffocated by too much compromise, unless one of the partners has some Oldest or Youngest traits.

- If both are Youngests, their marriage may be lots of fun, but who's in control? Their relationship could get out of hand if no one is minding the store.

- An Oldest marrying a Youngest could be a very good combination. Oldest can organize the Youngest, who can teach the Oldest that it's okay to have fun. Jack is an Oldest; Margaret a Youngest.

- If Oldest marries Middler, they are generally more successful in making lasting marriages. The Middler can compromise with strong-willed Oldest.

- If Middle marries Youngest, Middler could be drawn into the fun-loving life style of Youngest. The combination works better if the Middler has some Oldest traits.

What effects might birth order have on the marriages in the second JacMar generation? JJ seems to be a true Oldest and is married to Judy, an only child who is a trial lawyer. Does it seem that there may be some unhealthy competition in that shaky marriage?

Frank is a Middler, Frances a Youngest. Frances's compulsive spending has been a big factor in their financial dilemma. Frank is a consummate "good ol' boy," a pleaser. Has Frank been drawn into financial irresponsibility by Frances's fun-loving indulgences with their children?

Karen is a post-five-year gap Oldest, Kenneth a Youngest.

From the birth-order standpoint, this may be a good combination. Kenneth can help Karen loosen up, and Karen may help Kenneth keep things tidy.

Not all psychologists agree on the importance of birth order, but it's hard to ignore the argument that there is at least some significance. Consider:

- Charles Darwin was the youngest son in four generations of youngest sons.

- Benjamin Franklin was the youngest son in five generations of youngest sons.

- It is said that the American character is shaped by younger sons. The oldest sons stayed in Europe to guard their inheritances.

Inside Your Business Family . . .

Review the birth order in your family of origin. Based strictly on birth order, do members of your family resemble the personality types described in this chapter? If not, how are they different? How would you explain the differences?

Now check the birth orders of the married couples in your family of origin and in your spouse's family. Based strictly on birth order, how do these couples resemble the couples discussed in the chapter?

4

RESTLESS SUCCESSORS AND UNSPOKEN OPINIONS

My brother, Fred Hoenberg, very clearly wants to take over the company. He knows that, she knows that, and I know that.
—*David Hochberg, Vice President Public Relations,*
Lillian Vernon Corporation[4]

In his autobiography, Stanley Marcus of the famous Neiman-Marcus retailing empire discloses one of his greatest disappointments in life: Stanley's father didn't name him president of Neiman-Marcus on his fortieth birthday. Stanley's peers in public companies were becoming presidents. Stanley had to wait until his family was ready for him to lead them.

JJ

JJ, also age forty, shares Stanley Marcus's frustration. JJ has worked for the family business since completing his MBA degree eighteen years ago. He has never worked elsewhere. JJ is intelligent and hardworking, but he's not like his father. JJ doesn't have "charisma," he has a management mentality. He is neither genius nor hero; he is persistent, tough minded, and analytical.

Father and Son—Management Styles

His father views work as *psychodrama*. JJ sees work as a *process* in which people and ideas are combined to make decisions. By negotiating, bargaining, rewarding, and punishing, JJ limits the choices of those who work for him.

Jack is forever exciting his people to do new things in new ways. Jack relates to people intuitively, empathically.

JJ pays more attention to *how* things get done. Jack keeps his eye on *what* gets done.

JJ communicates with employees by sending *signals*. One of his strongest signals is that some day he will run JacMar Corporation and things will be different. Signals are ambiguous, can always be reinterpreted. Employees don't always know where JJ is coming from or what he wants. Jack communicates by *messages* that generate emotional responses from his people, although they don't always like what they hear. Jack has intense relationships with his people.

JJ is more distant. Responsibility for accounting and computer operations fulfill JJ's need for structure and order. The chaos his father creates drives JJ bananas! Jack speaks in rich emotional content evoking turbulent feelings of identity, difference, love or hate. It's win-or-lose with Jack.

JJ relates to people according to the role they play in getting the job done. His goal is win-win for everyone. JJ tries to solve problems before they arise, forever accosting people with "what-ifs," generated by spreadsheets.

JJ's MBA management style doesn't wear well with Jack. He comes across as distant, even cold. How would JJ motivate technical people? He's not an engineer. So who would generate the ideas? In Jack's mind, JacMar Corporation is like no other business. There are no comparisons. No one is capable of running the company but Jack, and Jack is running out of time!

Frank

Frank, age thirty-eight, is the consummate "good ol' boy." Warm, friendly, funny—Frank is JacMar's sales manager.

Like his older brother, Frank's entire working career has been with the family business. Unlike his brother, Frank never finished college. In the second semester of his sophomore year, Frank was fed up with school. He asked his father for a job. "Certainly not!" was Jack's quick reply. "No son of mine is going to work for this company without a college degree. And it ought to be an engineering degree!" Margaret intervened. To refuse Frank a job would be like rejecting him from the family. "No son of ours is going to be rejected by this family!" said Margaret. Frank was hired.

Frank has an unusual, if effective, work style. Frank had to find a way out. He just couldn't work in the office with his father—Jack was always on him about something, always criticizing. Frank couldn't seem to please him. So Frank, a three-handicap golfer, handles most of his sales responsibilities while playing golf with customers. And Frank has been extraordinarily successful. Annual sales are now in the $30 million range.

Outsiders can't understand why Jack seems so hard on his gentle, likable son, Frank. Some of it has to do with Frank's striking physical resemblance to Jack's alcoholic father—and to Frank's two convictions for driving while intoxicated. (Frank, however, is not an alcoholic, and the DWI convictions happened years ago.) Jack never drinks; never has. Jack's father was known as a "happy drunk" in the 1940s, which accounts for why he worked only intermittently; why he contributed so little income to the household. Jack thinks he sees his father's weakness in Frank. And Jack can't deal with it.

Karen

Daughter Karen, at age twenty-nine, is seven years younger than Frank. Karen is very bright, energetic, and a graduate engineer.

She works for a large avionics company on the West Coast. Karen has been spotted as a "comer" by those she reports to, and by those who report to her.

In many ways Karen resembles her father. She has blinding energy, a creative mind, and the ability to inspire technical people. But Karen is still Jack's "little girl." Within earshot of Karen, Jack once told a friend, "For a *woman*, Karen's not a bad engineer." Karen knows how much Jack wants her to have children and to "come home." Jack has always assured Karen that whomever she marries will have a good job with JacMar Corporation. But Jack has never offered Karen a job.

JJ would have mixed feelings about his sister's return to JacMar Corporation. Karen would certainly bring needed engineering talent, but she might also be a contender to succeed Jack as CEO. And that would be threatening to JJ, especially in light of his parents' current estate plan.

Inside Your Business Family . . .

Describe the work style of your business leader. Is his or her work style more like Jack's or like JJ's? Describe the work style of the heir-apparent successor to your business leader. Compare the heir-apparent's work style with that of your business leader. Are they compatible in the business?

Will your heir-apparent's present work style be successful as he or she leads the company? Should he or she make some work-style changes? If so, what changes?

How are "signals" and "messages" sent and received in your company?

As you read about the relationships between Jack and his three children, what parallel situations come to mind in your family?

What different situations come to mind in your family?

Do younger-generation members of your family still compete with each other? If so, how? Is the level of competition in your family healthy?

5

GENERATIONAL ISSUES

The problem with most children of entrepreneurs is that they want to compete with their parents. They want to be richer, have bigger businesses, do it quicker.
—*David Hochberg, Vice President/Public Relations,*
Lillian Vernon Corporation[5]

Some say the most common tensions between older and younger generations in business together involve *power* and *control*. The older generation wants continued domination, the younger generations wants independence and clout. The older generation wants to hang in there, the younger generation wants them to let go.

The best way to understand these generational tensions in the business setting, and how to deal with them, begins by understanding the life cycles of the family members involved. Harvard psychologist David Levenson has identified a number of life stages common to most men and women that more or less relate to chronological age. Some stages are relatively smooth. Others can be upsetting and stressful.

How fathers and their children get along in business together at any given time may depend on where they are in their respective life cycles. The bulk of available research deals with fathers and sons. What is known about the quality of father-daughter business relationships is important, but fragmentary, and needs further study and data.

FATHERS AND SONS

Let's begin with fathers and sons. Researchers have measured the quality of father-son relationships by the ease of their interaction at work, their enjoyment of work relationships, how much they accomplish, and how much they learn from each other. They conclude that seven factors strongly influence the quality of father-son work relationships:

- agreement on the formal purpose of their work relationship

- how much clarity and overlap exist in their mutual responsibilities

- the type and level of power exercised by each

- similarities and differences in their objectives, activities, traits, and work styles

- the degree of affection each holds for the other

- the costs and benefits each receive from working together, as measured against work expectations and alternatives

- their ability and willingness to send and receive messages

Levenson's research identifies ages thirty-five to forty-five as a turbulent life stage. He calls it the "deadline decade," when men begin to sense that all of their dreams won't come true, that their options are fewer, that they are mortal and finite, that their time is running out. Deadliners may not even know what they want when they "grow up," and are sensitive to transition in their families as their children grow up and leave home.

Deadliners and Individuation

Most young men (and women) in their late teens and early twenties are still in the process of separating from their families, seeking their own identities, becoming their own persons. Psychologists call this separation from the family process, "individuation." Energies and drives are at a high point. When Jack was forty-five and JJ was twenty-two, Jack was a "deadliner"; JJ was "individuating," still full of fresh memories of childhood and adolescent conflicts with his father. A young man in this first midlife crisis who leaves high school or college to go to work for his father submits himself to Dad's control over his life at the very time he can least tolerate it. Because JJ had outside career opportunities, he felt little need to make their work relationship succeed and resented any perceived pressure to join JacMar Corporation. With limited responsibilities and closely supervised by his father, JJ felt oversupervised and held back. He also felt isolated from other employees, who were suspicious or resentful of his advantages as Jack's son. JJ desperately needed the approval of his peers. However, what he heard was distorted.

Having entered the business directly from college, wrapped in an MBA degree, JJ was eager to put his new "book knowledge" to work. Schooling had encouraged JJ to question his father's proven methods, but it had also failed to prepare him to accept his place in JacMar Corporation. Jack took many of his son's suggestions for change as personal criticism and rejected most of them on emotional grounds. Jack didn't appreciate the freedom of thought and discussion JJ had enjoyed in the classroom.

During the deadline decade, entrepreneurs may strive to give their lives meaning that will live on after them. Fathers feel acutely their sons' challenges to their authority during this period. Indeed, a son's challenges may underscore a father's questions about his own identity and threaten his sense of control. In this second midlife crisis, Jack redoubled his efforts to leave his personal stamp on JacMar Corporation and strongly asserted his power over others. He had little patience with anyone who questioned him, especially JJ. Those questions only reinforced Jack's self-doubt and threatened his control.

Jack at forty-five and JJ at twenty-two were both questioning their identities, reappraising their lives. The quality of their work relationship suffered for a time. Since each man was emotionally charged, each distorted the messages the other sent. Each felt threatened by the other's actions and needs. Their communication during this period was predictably poor.

On the other hand, when Jack was fifty-four and JJ thirty-one, the turbulence between them seemed to subside. The years between forty-five and sixty are good ones for most men; they are less competitive than before, feel less pressed to condemn others, less controlled by external forces. They value possessions less, seem more objective, more philosophical about life and its demands. They are better able to respond to the needs of their children and young adults, more willing to teach and mentor. This describes Jack at fifty-four.

The years for young men between twenty-three and twenty-eight might not be particularly stable. Men in these years are concerned with keeping their options open, but inside they want stability. Outside they feel pressured to grow up, find a direction, get married, to test their identity in relationships. From twenty-eight to thirty-three, most men focus on the direction of their lives with some urgency, reappraising the past and scrutinizing the future. By age thirty-three, most have made their principal occupational choice and have committed their lives to that decision. Settled into career choices, they feel more secure, become more materialistic, increasingly concerned with recognition and advancement.

At ages fifty-four and thirty-one, respectively, the quality of work relationships between Jack and JJ had stabilized. Their communications had become less emotional. Now committed to the family business, JJ determined to make the best of his relationship with his father. Since Jack was less materialistic during this period, he seemed more attuned to JJ's material needs. Jack and JJ felt that the rewards, recognition, responsibilities, and authority were fairly divided between them.

Jack and JJ Today

Today, Jack is sixty-three and JJ is forty. Between sixty and sixty-five, there tends to be a replay of the deadline decade: Friends begin to die. Retirement looms for men who have always equated work with life. Entrepreneurs, who plan never to retire, seem compelled to demonstrate their dominance over others during this phase of their lives. The free enterprise system has rewarded them with the freedom *not* to retire.

Men between thirty-five and forty-five typically strive for competence, recognition, advancement, and security. Some call this the Becoming One's Own Man (BOOM) period. Between thirty-five and forty-five, a man may urgently seek independence and recognition. This sense of urgency can provoke a resurgence of the "little boy" in the man. He may relive some elemental struggles with dependence, sexuality, and authority. Relationships with wives and mentors can be stormy.

The resurgence of strong emotions about dependence on Jack stimulates very negative attitudes in JJ—at times a lack of trust. The quality of the relationship between Jack and JJ suffers because of what's going on inside both of them. JJ's struggle with authority overlaps Jack's need to demonstrate his continuing value to JacMar Corporation. Their respective emotional states have seriously distorted communication between them.

JJ's drive to take charge clashes with Jack's strong instinct to dig in. There are serious conflicts about the direction of the company: Jack wants to maintain a steady course, JJ wants to experiment, innovate, change. JJ complains that his father no longer updates him on what's happening and retains the final say. Because he thinks that some other career options are still open to him, however limited, JJ feels comfortable in challenging his father. These tensions are especially intense because Jack has failed to delegate decision-making authority to JJ.

Can they get along?

Anticipating Changes

The most important lesson is that *changes like these can be anticipated*. Fathers and sons should expect their relationships to change over time, as each develops and matures. The more they recognize this inevitable change, the less likely they will blame each other for their clashes. Fathers and sons need to cultivate the ability to see themselves objectively, to acknowledge their own feelings.

Ideally, JJ should have joined JacMar Corporation only after both he and his father were beyond their periods of identity formation. Had JJ entered the business at age thirty, his father would have been fifty-three, clear of the deadline decade.

Ultimately, the responsibility for getting along lies with both men. Their areas of responsibility should be separated, each given final authority to make decisions in his own domain. "All-or-nothing" arguments should be avoided. Otherwise, JJ may suspect that he must have his father completely out of his life in order to control his own destiny. It's much more important for JJ to escape Jack's shadow and reach than to displace Jack completely. Joint exercise of *real responsibility* is the key to their future relationship. But Jack holds the trump card. Jack's emotional attachment to JacMar Corporation competes with his emotional attachment to JJ.

Jack must decide which child means more to him: JJ or JacMar Corporation.

FATHERS AND DAUGHTERS

Psychologist Collette Dumas interviewed a number of fathers and daughters in business together. Her report, "Understanding

Father-Daughter and Father-Son Dyads in Family-Owned Businesses,"[6] summarizes those interviews and points out some clear, gender-based differences in work styles and work relationships. Professor Dumas did not undertake a statistical analysis of daughters who become CEOs of family companies. Rather, she sought to identify those factors that signify gender differences in the succession process.

Daughters' identities in the business were quite ambiguous, ranging from "daddy's little girl" to tough-minded independence. Sometimes the daughter joined the business to "take care" of her father, by being his listener, admirer, and supporter. Taking care didn't include competing with the father for control of the business—a common pattern between sons and fathers. Most daughters were struggling with "who they were" in the business environment, and most looked to their fathers as role models. Asserting themselves, disagreeing, or arguing with their fathers was very difficult. Upon realizing their own strengths and their fathers' weakness, they felt guilty—a loss of innocence.

For their brothers, the struggle with their fathers was for autonomy, for becoming one's own man. For daughters, the struggle became maintaining intimacy—finding ways to continue to be joined with their fathers, rather than separated. Whereas sons typically view themselves as potential successors, daughters don't. *Not one of the fathers Dumas interviewed considered his daughter as a potential successor*—nor, barring unforeseen crisis, did any of the daughters.

Dumas observed a novel triangular tension among fathers, daughters, and unrelated managers. In some instances daughters sought to protect their fathers against "bad managers," while in others managers sought to protect the father against "bad daughters." Dumas didn't find a similar triangulation among fathers, sons, and managers, although she did find one among fathers, daughters, and mothers, which she called the "Snow White Syndrome." In those instances, the daughter joined the business in an attempt to manage a lack of closeness with her mother.

Overall, Dumas found significantly less conflict between daughters and fathers than between sons and fathers. But the majority of daughters admitted to being restless in their caretaker roles. They felt they had no voice, were forced to take a position of inferiority to their brothers, had no real identity in the business, were unable to take charge—all because they were women.

Dumas warns that it is dangerous for advisors to assume that daughters in business are no different from sons. Daughters' particular needs and roles need to be considered separately, and she suggests ways to avoid daughters' "invisibility" in the business. Daughters need official recognition of their status on the organization chart, with appropriate titles and challenging, written job descriptions—including their responsibilities as decision makers. She urges paying particular attention to frustrating "triangles" with managers and mothers.

By securing employment elsewhere, Karen spared JacMar Corporation some of these gender concerns. But other gender concerns lie perilously close to the surface in the JacMar family.

Inside Your Business Family . . .

Examine the father-son relationships in your family business in light of the seven factors presented on the first page of this chapter. Write down the ages of the men in your business. How do the descriptions of what's going on *inside* Jack and JJ at various ages compare to what's going on inside the men in your family business and the men discussed in this chapter?

How do the relationships between Jack and JJ at various ages correspond to the relationships between the men in your family business at these ages? What changes in these relationships have you observed over the past few years? Are these changes positive, negative, or mixed? What changes should be made in these relationships?

Examine the mother-daughter, mother-son, and father-daughter relationships in your busines family in light of the factors presented on the first page of this chapter. Write down the ages of the women in your family business.

In light of Professor Dumas's research, ask each of the same questions posed above about the mother-daughter, mother-son, and father-daughter relationships in your business. How are the relationships similar? How are they different?

It is said that the lifelong issues between parents and children are power and control, that the lifelong issue between siblings is fairness. Do you agree?

6

THE FAMILY AND THE FUTURE

Most of the companies that make women's underwear are run by men, so why shouldn't a woman run a men's underwear company?

—Donna Wolf Steigerwaldt, Chairman,
Jockey International, Inc.[7]

In 1986, JacMar Corporation elected to be taxed as an S Corporation. There is one class of shares, all common, all voting. Jack and Margaret each own 41 percent; the three children each own 5 percent, all annual gifts from their parents. The remaining three percent is owned by the general manager, Al, who is not related.

Since the beginning, Margaret insisted on owning a significant number of shares. Margaret's upbringing was much more comfortable than Jack's. Her family owned a business that made it through the Great Depression, but the business passed to her two older brothers. She was never consulted, never considered as an owner or an employee. Margaret sees herself as a victim of the "Honey, don't worry your pretty little head" school of chauvinism. She was hurt deeply at being ignored by her father and brothers and is still very angry about it.

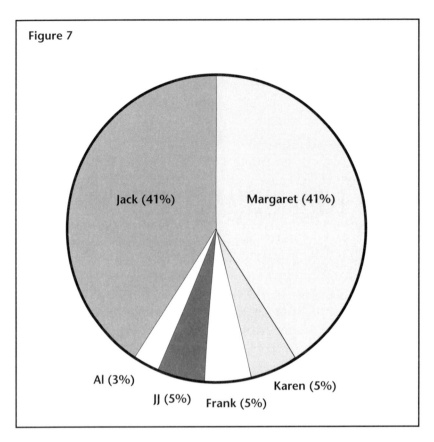

Figure 7

Jack (41%)

Margaret (41%)

Al (3%)

JJ (5%)   Frank (5%)

Karen (5%)

THE ESTATE PLAN

Jack and Margaret dream of passing JacMar Corporation to their three children. Under their present estate plan, the children will each own one-third of the company stock after both parents have died. After the first parent dies, his or her stock is placed in a trust to postpone the federal estate tax until the surviving parent dies. If Jack dies first, the estate plan names Margaret as trustee of a trust holding Jack's 41 percent of the stock. Margaret would control JacMar Corporation for the remainder of her life.

The sons know about the estate plan and are troubled. Margaret is in excellent health; her life expectancy is at least twenty more years. This means that JJ and Frank could be in their sixties before they gain control of JacMar Corporation. Her sons aren't sure how Margaret would exercise her control: Would she take a direct hand in running the company? Would she name herself as CEO? Might she name Karen as Jack's successor, giving Karen the role that was denied to Margaret by her own family's business?

Karen is also concerned about the estate plan. She certainly has no intentions of returning to JacMar Corporation while her father is alive (Karen and Jack are probably too much alike to coexist in the same company). Moreover, she hasn't been invited. Karen likes her West Coast job and has recently married Kenneth, also an engineer with her company. Karen has mixed feelings about inheriting her third of JacMar Corporation. What would she do with the stock? Vote her shares to break ties when her brothers can't agree? Receive little or no dividends in excess of her share of the S corporation taxes? Wonder constantly how her brothers are "plundering" the company with high salaries and lavish perks? Of course, Karen doesn't want to appear ungrateful—but couldn't her parents leave her something else? Some publicly traded stocks? Even life insurance?

THE IN-LAWS

Whether husbands or wives, whether they work in the company or not, spouses are always key players in a business family. Once upon a time, Margaret and Jack came to an unspoken agreement that Jack would be in charge of family thinking and Margaret in charge of family feelings. Of course they never negotiated or discussed it; it just happened over time. This was a common division of family responsibility between couples in their generation.

During the early days, Margaret felt obliged to work at JacMar Corporation—to do those jobs Jack couldn't or wouldn't do. Working there was like paying her dues for the faith she had in him. Jack wouldn't have launched the business without

Margaret's encouragement. Yet, like many other entrepreneurial wives of her generation, when Jack hired someone to fill her place, Margaret moved back home and fired the housekeeper. Though Margaret hasn't worked for JacMar Corporation since the early days, Jack talks to her about important business decisions. Margaret has strong opinions and favors Jack with them. Although he may pretend to ignore them, Jack values Margaret's views. Indeed, a few years ago, Jack was offered $20 million for JacMar Corporation. When he brought the exciting news to Margaret, she burst into tears. "Jack, how could you sell the company after all the sacrifices *we* have made?!"

Margaret remains a powerful player (remember how she prevailed when Frank asked for a job?) and will play a central role in deciding who will succeed Jack. Like many other spouses of founders, Margaret is the "chief emotional officer" of JacMar Corporation. If she wished, Margaret could disrupt or change any plan for succession.

Judy

Judy, married to JJ, is a trial lawyer. They have one child, Jack III, who is eight years old. Judy, at forty, is unlikely to have more children. Judy's relationship with her father-in-law is not good. Judy talks business with men all week long, but Jack refuses to discuss *his* business with her. She takes Jack's silence as a chauvinist slight, which is partly true.

But Jack has another reason. He knows that the marriage between Judy and JJ has been shaky. If their marriage doesn't make it, he doesn't want JacMar stock falling into Judy's hands in a property settlement. JacMar's lawyers have recommended a buy-sell agreement for some time that would require any family member desiring to sell JacMar stock to offer it first to other family members pro rata. The lawyers drafted one proposal several years ago that would have fixed the price for intrafamily stock sales at the book value of the company—a price considerably lower that the shares were worth at the time. Judy refused to sign.

Frances

Frank's wife, Frances, is a genuine "earth mother." Their four children range in ages from eighteen to twelve. Frances is a warm, lovable person—a middle child like her husband. She, too, is interested in the business and has tried to talk to Jack about it even though she doesn't understand business. The hitch is that Frances doesn't know that she doesn't understand. When she asks Jack about the business, he teases her, toys with her lack of knowledge. Frances may not understand business, but she does know when she's being ridiculed and is hurt and offended by Jack's humiliating antics.

Kenneth

Kenneth is an engineer. Like Karen, he has been spotted as a "comer" in the avionics company that employs them both. Jack likes to discuss engineering problems with Kenneth, though Karen isn't included in their conversations. Kenneth's folk hero is August Busch, Mr. Anheuser's son-in-law who made the Budweiser brewing family a fortune. Kenneth admires Jack greatly. Kenneth's father is Al, JacMar's general manager.

RELATIONSHIPS

All things considered, Judy and Frances get along pretty well with Margaret and with each other. Kenneth is still an unknown quantity—is he a potential rival to JJ and Frank?

There has always been sibling rivalry between JJ and Frank, who have competed all their lives to please their strong-willed father. The brothers maintain a healthy distance, JJ in the office and Frank on the golf course, which helps keep their rivalry in check. JacMar pays them identical salaries, bonuses, and perks. JJ grumbles that he should earn more because he is older and next in line for CEO. Frank grumbles because he has college-age children and thinks his compensation should take this into account. Margaret insists that the sons be paid exactly the same. Karen thinks both are paid too much.

Inside Your Business Family . . .

Who would control *your* company after the present business leader dies? Would this successor ownership cause problems? If so, what problems?

Do you understand why Margaret feels the way she does about JacMar Corporation? Are there members of your family with similar feelings? Does your family have a "chief emotional officer"? Who will succeed him or her?

Are there times or circumstances when your *family values* and your *business values* clash? How has your family handled these tensions?

Is chauvinism present in your family? Which women are affected? Which men are the primary offenders? What is your family doing about it?

Are siblings separated in your family business? By location? By job responsibilities? By other means?

Which family members are being paid more than they are "worth"? Less?

7

TODAY AND TOMORROW

I keep telling them I've got to retire, and they keep finding more things for me to do.
—*Eileen Ford, President and Director, Ford Models, Inc.*[8]

Like many business owners with adult children on staff, Jack feels fairly healthy and energetic but not ready to let go of the business he has spent a lifetime building. In Jack's mind, the kids will have plenty of time to run the business after he retires (an event he has given little thought to) or dies (an event he has given *no* thought to).

For entrepreneurs like Jack, work is life, retirement is death. Jack wants to postpone any withdrawal from JacMar Corporation—the living monument to his success. He wants to savor his accomplishments. The children will have plenty of time to enjoy the company on their own.

LETTING GO

His sons are frustrated. In giving them fancy titles and overgenerous salaries, Jack was hoping to keep them satisfied, at least for a few years. However, neither brother has significant bottom-line authority, and their titles and their fat paychecks only rein-force their doubts about self-worth.

So Jack and JJ need to talk; Jack has no idea of the extent of his elder son's frustration. Both men have legitimate needs that seem to conflict, but they don't have to consider an all-or-noth-ing scenario. Jack doesn't have to retire today, but he does need to find areas of the business where JJ can assume control. Here are some suggestions:

- If Jack wants to retire eventually, he can take off one extra day a week each year until he is phased out completely. In seven years (no, not five—he has been working seven days a week) Jack will be out for good.

- Make Al (his current general manager) the transition CEO to take over some of Jack's duties and eventually to pass them along to JJ. Meanwhile, JJ could take charge of all new projects and ventures.

- If Jack wants to stay in the saddle, he could revise the orga-nization chart so that no more than five people report to him. Everyone else should report to JJ.

Karen and the family need to talk. They need to discuss Karen's "today" needs. They need to know that Karen wants to start her own family, that Kenneth wants to earn his MBA degree, that Karen would like to tap JacMar Corporation for the money to finance their needs.

There is a basic obstacle to Jack letting go, however. Most of Jack and Margaret's net worth—over 90 percent—is tied up in JacMar Corporation. Their future financial security depends upon the company's continuing success. To let go is to risk their retirement security. With genuine doubts about their sons' abili-ties, they feel trapped into hanging on. To turn JacMar Corporation over to their sons would make them dependent upon their sons' unproven abilities. In a real sense, letting go would violate Rule One of estate planning: never make parents dependent upon their children.

There is a further obstacle that is built in to most business families.

Inside Your Business Family . . .
Are "todays" and "tomorrows" conflicting in your family business?

Does your business leader have concrete retirement plans? If so, are they realistic? Have these retirement plans been shared with the family? With key employees?

What kinds of financial needs are your younger generation members facing? Which of these financial needs do you consider legitimate?

Is your business leader financially dependent on the future success of the business? Would letting go, stepping back, make him or her financially dependent on the next generation?

Part Two

THE 39 CRITICAL QUESTIONS

8

COMMITMENT

Our contemporaries from college and graduate school are hopping from company to company or are moving up in a fast-growing company, and they've outpaced us in terms of salary. It is ironic but I think we're all aware that in the long run, we'll be better off.

—*David Crane, President Excelsior Printing Co.*[9]

Critical Question 1: *Are we committed to the future of our family business?*

Critical Question 2: *Are we obligated to work there indefinitely, or may we pursue other careers?*

A family business can be a powerful *symbol*. The company can symbolize family accomplishment, family heritage, family power, family standing in the eyes of the community and the world. But it's not worthwhile to plan for the future of the family business if no one really *wants* it. Yet in many business families, future commitment to the business is never discussed, it is just *assumed*. Older generation owners plan meticulously to give their children what they think the children *ought to* want. Most don't talk with the children about what the children *really* want.

But this dilemma goes deeper. Children reared in business

families often feel an unspoken obligation to work in the business. Not to work in the business would disappoint their parents; not to work in the business would appear ungrateful for the comfortable and privileged life the business has offered them.

For the founder or business leader, the company is likely a deep psychological symbol of self-worth, self-esteem, of meaning in life. For a second-, third-, or fourth-generation business leader, the business is a link with family heritage and with loved ones long dead. The eldest son may feel particularly sensitive to an unspoken or implied obligation to continue the business.

SIGNALS AND MESSAGES

People communicate through both *signals* and *messages*. Signals are ambiguous; they don't carry specific meaning—in fact, sometimes they *obscure* what the speaker means. Messages state a clear position. They heighten emotional responses, and increase the likelihood that the hearer won't like what he hears.

"Someday this will all be yours" may be a signal by which a father really means, "You can have what's left of this sucker when I can no longer put my feet on the floor." "Someday this will all be yours" may send the message that the hearer is expected to take over. Or, "Someday this will all be yours" may carry the signal that Father hasn't decided when or how to transfer the mantle.

The older business leader is basking, savoring the fruits of his success. The *message* is clear: "Our family name is on the vans, the water tower, the letterhead. By Golly, I built it, and I'm going to enjoy it!" "Today, today, today" is the older generation's preoccupation, because "tomorrow" is quite problematical. Meanwhile the younger generation frets in frustration. The signal they receive is, "Wait, prepare, train, get ready." But there is no timetable, no career path, no succession plan. No wonder they ask, but not aloud, "Are we committed to the future of our family business, when the future is so obscure?"

Children of privileged families seem to have endless options these days. With good educations, money behind them, and a global economy, the career varieties open to them are mind-boggling.

They are impatient, ready to get on with their lives! Why should children of privilege wallow in frustration trying to sort out ambiguous signals about their limited options in the family business?

Well, love and loyalty to the family are powerful reasons to wait it out. A child who rejects a future in the family business could be viewed as renouncing a place in the family tradition and heritage, as rejecting the lifetime accomplishments of ancestors, of being disloyal to kin.

But this position cuts both ways.

The child who is *not* offered a future in the family business may feel outcast: Why am I not permitted to take a place in the family heritage and tradition? Why am I rejected by the family? Why is the older generation being disloyal by not including me in its future plans? Does someone doubt my commitment to the family? Has someone decided I'm *disloyal*?!

Probably not, but keep in mind a fundamental truth: A parent who keeps silent is almost always assumed to disapprove. Silence = disapproval.

Are we—founder and successor, parent and child—*both* committed to the future of our family business? Or do we assume lack of commitment from our silence?

Got the message?

Commitment to the future of the business and willingness to work there indefinitely must *not* be assumed. Commitment (or the lack of it) must be discussed and dealt with—like *all* of the Critical Questions.

Inside Your Business Family . . .

Is there an unspoken obligation, in your family, to go into the family business?

What does your business symbolize? Heritage? Tradition? Power? Public approval?

What does "Someday this will all be yours" mean in your family?

What other options are open to younger generation members of your family who *don't* go into the business? How long will (or should) they wait for a clear picture of their futures in the business?

What other powerful unstated assumptions exist in your family?

9

KEEP OR SELL?

The companies we've been attempting to sell off, to get into cash, we've done that in most cases. Now I'm sitting on a pile of money and we hope maybe to make some investments, but I have no idea where those investments will be made.

—*Marshall Field V, Field Corporation*[10]

Critical Question 3: *Do we want to own the business or should it be sold?*

Some families don't discuss selling the family business. It would be unthinkable, like Esau selling his birthright to Jacob.

Some outside advisors believe that selling the business would eliminate unpleasantness, conflict, alienation, intrigue, rivalry.

Some families threaten to sell the business if certain family members don't behave in acceptable ways or don't find a way to get along. But the threat is seldom carried out.

Jack doesn't want to sell JacMar Corporation. The company is his life work, his favorite child, his self. Margaret doesn't want to sell JacMar Corporation. The company symbolizes her husband's success, her family's accomplishment, their respected place in the world. For Jack, the offer of $20 million for JacMar

Corporation was exciting and close to Jack's price. For Margaret the offer was reassuring but threatening—hence her tearful response to Jack, "How could you sell this company we have worked so hard to build?!" It would be easier to consider a sale if none of their children worked for the company, if none of the children aspired to own the company some day.

There is another consideration that Jack and Margaret haven't discussed—their future financial security. With more than 90 percent of the couple's net worth vested in JacMar, Jack and Margaret's financial security is tied to the company's continuing success. Neither is sure it would prosper without Jack at the helm. Selling the company now—cashing out—would certainly alleviate their financial concerns about the future.

A "WALK THROUGH"

Jack and Margaret attended a family business seminar presented by a large bank. The seminar speakers encouraged business families to "walk through" the sale of their business. According to the bankers, a walk through meant finding out:

- whether your company is salable

- who might buy it

- what price you might expect

The seminar speakers pointed out their options related to sales, such as dividing the business between family groups; selling the business to younger generation members (instead of them waiting to inherit); buying out shareholders who aren't active in the business; strategic sales of minority shares to outsiders; selling to employees or to an employee stock-ownership plan; or even going public. Jack made a mental note that JJ and Frank might be interested in buying their parents' stock, but this would require that the sons borrow a great deal of money and that Jack and Margaret pay capital gains taxes on the sale. Nevertheless, a sale to their sons is one way to provide the financial security Jack and Margaret seek while keeping JacMar Corporation in the family.

During the question time, Jack asked how a business family might find a suitable buyer. The speaker suggested that the ultimate buyer would probably be a total stranger. He further suggested that JacMar hire a reputable business broker (who may be an investment banker) who is qualified to guide the family through a sale. If they decide to sell, the broker can value the business, help find a buyer, and negotiate the deal.

The speaker cautioned Jack and Margaret that, at some point, the broker will want some assurance they are serious about selling, since the broker's fees are contingent upon the sale going through. If they are undecided about a sale, they could hire a broker to walk the family through the process, but they should tell the broker up front that they are undecided and negotiate the broker's fee arrangement on that basis. "The broker may discover weaknesses in your business, or may discover value you didn't know was there," the speaker commented. He concluded, "Keeping your business 'fixed up to sell' is probably a good idea."

That sounded like good advice to Jack. Walking through a sale would help him get a fresh perspective on JacMar Corporation. A broker or investment banker might spot weaknesses he had overlooked; might identify some of his shortsightedness in management; or might illuminate long-standing arguments about the profitability of certain lines or projects.

Jack has always been curious to know how an appraiser would value his company. He knows a thorough appraisal would be expensive—from $5,000 to $50,000—but his hesitation has been due more to the fear the Internal Revenue Service would find a way to use the appraiser's report against him for tax purposes than to the fee. "Not a problem," counsels Jack's lawyer. "Let me order it. The attorney-client privilege will protect the appraiser's report from the prying eyes of the IRS." Jack and Margaret also discussed other aspects of a sale with their lawyers.

Jack talked with a number of friends who had sold their businesses. He gleaned the following from these conversations:

- A buyer would want all of the stock. The other shareholders—the children and Al, the general manager—would need to agree to the sale.

- A large company might be willing to acquire JacMar Corporation in exchange for its shares. If so, the sale could be tax free. The sellers' tax basis in JacMar Corporation would carry over to the shares received. However, securities regulations might require the JacMars to keep those shares for a minimum of two years after the transaction.

- The purchaser of JacMar Corporation would probably require that Jack continue in a consulting capacity for several years after the sale. Although Jack would be well paid for his consulting services, the buyer might not follow his advice.

- The new owner might make some management changes against Jack's better judgment, or discharge employees who had served Jack long and faithfully. Jack might disapprove of changes in product quality or in customer service, but he would be powerless to overrule them.

- JJ and Frank might be invited to continue, but only so long as their job performance satisfied the new owner. Being the sons of a prior owner would give them little advantage.

- The new owner might view JacMar Corporation strictly as an investment. The mixture of family trust, love, and loyalty in the business would disappear. The assets might be stripped away and the business closed. The company might be resold or lose its identity in a merger with other companies. The buyer's primary concern is profitability, its measuring rod the discounted cash flow from the business.

To keep or to sell, that is the question.

Inside Your Business Family . . .

Has your family had a serious discussion about selling your business? Have there been recent *serious* approaches to buy your business? Was price discussed? Was an offer made? Was the offer discussed with the family? If so, what was the family's reaction? If your business were sold, what family problems would be solved? What problems would be created?

Go through the "keep or sell" exercise. Take a good look in the mirror—warts and all. Is there an existing appraisal of your business? What prompted that appraisal? Is that appraisal current? Is it realistic?

If your family were to walk through a sale of the business, how would various family members react to the process?

10

WHO'S IN AND WHO'S OUT?

Dad was the founder of the company, the leading philosopher and guiding light for us always. I'm not any of those things, and probably wouldn't be effective if I tried.
—*S. Robson Walton, Chairman, Wal-Mart Stores, Inc.*[11]

Critical Question 4: *How do we decide which family members will be employed by the company?*

Critical Question 5: *Must we offer every family member a job?*

Critical Question 6: *Should in-laws or other relatives be invited to work in the business?*

Critical Question 7: *What education or work preparation should be required of family members who work in the business?*

Critical Question 8: *How do we assign titles and work responsibility?*

Too often, business families practice "bird-cage management." Outside blood is rarely brought in to tackle tough business problems. The same family members, with the same limited skills and experiences, try to solve problems they couldn't solve before.

The "bird-cage" problem perpetuates itself every time another relative wants to join the firm. Instead of establishing *rules of entry*, the business owner shakes up the bird cage and forces everyone in the business to fly to a higher perch, willy-nilly, wherever they land.

THE BOSS'S KIDS

The dilemma began innocently enough with the children's first summer jobs as teenagers. JJ, Frank, and Karen became "the boss's kids," praised to their faces, but sometimes ridiculed behind their backs. Before long the children began wondering whether the other employees really liked them for themselves. Even today, JJ and Frank continue those uncertainties. More serious issues arose when the young family members chose a college, courses, majors, or graduate school. Jack made it clear he wanted each of them to study engineering at his alma mater. Otherwise, there were no ground rules about preparing for one's role in JacMar Corporation. JJ's primary interest was computer science, Karen adored engineering, and Frank just wanted to avoid school.

In some business families the rules of entry are very simple: Every family member who wants a job, gets a job. The bird cage is expanded to set a perch for everyone. Other businesses refuse to hire *any* family members, or at least require family members to compete for jobs and promotions on the same basis as other employees. None of the JacMar children knew the rules— because there weren't any.

ENTRY RULES

Each JacMar family member was handled as an individual case. The organization simply "made room" for each son as he came aboard. A case-by-case approach may work in the second generation, but usually breaks down in the third generation and beyond, when the sheer size of the family becomes unwieldy. All four of Frank's children are older than JJ's only child; Frank's oldest child, Frank Jr., is eighteen and in college, already making decisions about courses and major subjects, already wondering about a future role in JacMar Corporation. There are no entry rules to guide him.

Hiring family members mixes business and family issues at a very sensitive point. If entry is approached strictly as a business decision, only entry qualifications will be considered when Frank Jr. applies. This sounds good, but may be unrealistic. A mixed approach should work best, requiring a separate set of family rules for job entry. Entry rules begin with basic job qualifications: education, training, and experience. A family education requirement is crucial: too many college dropouts, such as Frank the elder, take refuge in a family business. Some may have learning disabilities, some may be uninterested in or unsuited for higher education, or they may be taking the easy way out of school. To discourage dropping out, some families impose educational requirements upon family members over and above those required by entry level job descriptions. For example, Frank Jr. may already meet the company's entry requirements as a junior bookkeeper, but *family* entry rules may also require an accounting degree.

WORKING ELSEWHERE

The JacMars might require a certain amount of time to elapse between education and entry into the business, say five years. So as to avoid a five-year "vacation" after college, there should be a further rule about minimum training and experience before entry. In some industries, there are formal training programs for the younger generation. Members of the Jewish Young Men's Apparel League, for example, hire each other's children for rigorous apprenticeships. Sons and daughters of independent Coca Cola bottlers often work for the Coca-Cola company or its subsidiaries before returning to the family operation. It's not so important for the younger generation to gain experience in the same industry as the family business. What is important is for them to fly or fall in a different bird cage, without the family safety net.

A most important reason for mandatory outside experience is self-esteem. Outside the family business, a child must face the traumas of transfer, promotion, termination, competition, evaluation, company politics—in other words, normal business life. Moreover, the young family member acquires skills, training, and experience that are simply unavailable to one who spends all of his or her working life in the family business. Of course, there are special situations—a child may be needed during economic reversals or because of the sudden death or disability of the founder or other key employee. It is also tempting to bend the rules when a child is divorced or laid off and badly needs a job. But by and large, a rule requiring significant outside experience is a good one.

Heading Off Problems

Entry rules that include working outside the company can prevent a great deal of misunderstanding and conflict, especially if the rules are fully discussed, written down, and circulated with good explanations. For example, a third-generation CEO will have to decide whether to employ any or all of eleven fourth-generation members. There are numerous nieces and nephews, as well as his own children; all are now teenagers. The parents of those teenagers (himself, his siblings, and his cousins) own significant shares in the company, though none except the CEO is active in management. Unless there are clear-cut family rules about entry into the business, he may be forced to decide on a case-by-case basis and is likely to offend some, if not all, of them.

This CEO is also looking ahead. He hopes his successor will be one of those fourth-generation teenagers. He hopes to shake the family bird cage and have the most qualified member fly to the top perch. As a result, he must look beyond mere entry to that future leader, whomever he or she is, needing experience and challenge outside the business in order to return and run it successfully. It might be a good short-term business decision to hire a talented but inexperienced family member to fill a job that is not particularly demanding. But a good, long-term business family decision would be to deny a nephew or niece that job until he or she acquires some outside experience that would help prepare him or her for eventual leadership. Working outside until age thirty seems about right. This allows the heir-apparent the next ten years, between thirty and forty, to prepare for succession. Tough love? Perhaps. But it is good business—or rather, good family business.

Making the Best Birdcage

The best family employment rules, like the best family decisions in other matters, are made when all participate, communicate, deliberate, and vote. Hammering out clear entry rules in an *intergenerational* forum leaves all family members feeling that they have been heard and treated fairly. Your goal is for everyone to feel like a winner in the process.

Family members who work in the business cannot escape the bird cage: It's always there.

Your challenge is to develop young birds who earn their wings.

THE FAMILY WELFARE STATE

Though politically and fiscally conservative, business families are prone to create a family welfare state with an elaborate system of benefits and privileges available to members of the gene pool, unrelated to merit or accomplishment. The family welfare state may be modest in first-generation business, but by the third generation, the family welfare state may have grown to unhealthy proportions. An "overclass" of family shareholders becomes more concerned with preserving and increasing entitlements—-dividends and perks—than with the growth and welfare of the company.

Giving and Withholding

Affluent business families worry about entitlements, about how much to give and how much to withhold from their children.

How much should we help them; how much should we require them to help themselves? Most business families offer children more help than they need—more than is healthy for them.

Business families generate two kinds of equity:

- *Sweat equity* is born of hard work and business acumen.

- *Blood equity* is acquired by gift, inheritance, or sheer indulgence.

Sweat equity is earned; blood equity comes by accident of birth.

Business families don't give themselves royal titles, though they do grant business titles, such as executive vice president (which means JJ is to stand and wait); or vice president of sales (for Frank, which means, "Let's sign this purchase order before we tee off on the back nine"). Most titles in business families don't jibe with real-work responsibility and inflate the bearer's worth to the company. Then there are empty titles: Karen is "Assistant Secretary," which means she signs the minutes of shareholder meetings (if they are held), the company pays her travel expenses to shareholder meetings, and she receives a check each month that wouldn't stand the scrutiny of an IRS agent.

Exaggerated titles indicate to others within the company and the community that a family member is more important than he or she really is. They also have more sinister potential: They sometimes delude the bearer of the title. His title as executive vice president (and the accompanying perks) induces JJ to throw his weight around the company. It embarrasses JJ when the world expects the clout that his title conveys and he can't deliver. Executive vice president or not, JJ can't yet sign company checks.

Entitlements are very much a part of business families.

Inside Your Business Family . . .

How did each of your family members enter the business? What were the circumstances? What were the rules? Who made the hiring decision? How was it made? How would clear entry rules have improved these decisions?

What are your company's current entry rules? What should they be? Who should make them? How should your family go about making them?

Outline an ideal set of entry rules for your family business.

Outline some recommendations for your family about outside work for those who aspire to work in the business.

Are "entitlements" a problem in your family business? Do any younger generation members behave like they have already inherited?

11

GROWING UP WEALTHY AND HEALTHY

I know there were times when she wished her name wasn't Wendy. When you name something after someone, that's a lot of responsibility.
                —*Dave Thomas, Founder, Wendy's International, Inc.*[12]

"Wealthy" can be an ambiguous word. To the JacMars, "wealthy" means a financial security that permits the indefinite continuation of their present life style without their having to work. But having wealth you didn't earn can cause problems. JJ and Frank remember when their father was struggling—when the family wasn't wealthy. Younger sister Karen doesn't have those memories; she has always known an affluent life style, takes it for granted, and assumes it will continue. Though they have not yet inherited from their parents, these three adult children are already beginning to think and act like inheritors.

SELF-ESTEEM, MATURITY, DISCIPLINE

It's hard for inheritors to value their own accomplishments. They are more likely to attribute their own successes to wealth and position than to good work on their own part. Inheritors are stung by others' resentment of their good fortune, and question whether they really are liked by others. Fear of failure runs high among inheritors, especially if their father has been a huge success. JJ and Frank have grown up in their father's shadow and are thought of as "his boys," though they are already middle-aged. Karen feels driven to make it on her own—in part to overcome her father's rejection.

A cocoon of wealth protects inheritors from life's challenges— "no pain, no gain" has no meaning for them. Most overprotected children do eventually grow up, but many delay or even avoid real maturity. It galls Jack that Frank spends so much time on the golf course, "like a kid." Then there are the drunk-driving convictions. In some ways, JJ and Frank still act like adolescents, particularly during disputes with their father.

Wealth makes it harder to stick to your goals in the face of setbacks and frustrations. Some inheritors' goals are ill-defined, particularly those involving career. Their motivations can be short-lived and lack intensity, since they are not driven by life's necessities. Frank is one of a legion of younger generation college dropouts who found refuge in the family business, where he didn't have to exercise self-discipline. For self-discipline requires focused and sustained energy, means postponing immediate gratification for higher rewards. Self-discipline seems incompatible with the silver spoon. Yet self-discipline is necessary not only for work but also for significant human relationships. Its lack is a lifelong source of difficulty. Jack thinks self-discipline requires sixty to seventy hours work each week. He is of the "old school" view that family members must work longer and harder than other employees to set a proper example. Heavily involved in civic activities, JJ works forty hours at most. If golf counts, Frank works respectable hours.

BOREDOM

Watch out for boredom if life is not very real or intense, if nothing matters that much. Lack of interest in life—*ennui*—leads to carelessness and irresponsibility in relationships. JJ fights boredom every day. His work is very frustrating—waiting, getting prepared, warming up, but never getting into the game. He desperately wants and needs bottom line responsibility at JacMar Corporation. Some of his work is interesting, but most days he leaves the office hassled on the outside and stressed on the inside.

POWER

Inheritors may feel uncomfortable with the power of their wealth since they haven't earned it. They may deny or avoid power. Or they may misuse it arbitrarily, running roughshod over other people—overcompensating for feelings of inadequacy and confusion. Either way, others find it hard to work for inheritors—and hard to live with them. JJ has had a hard time in the role of the boss's son. Too often JJ reminds other employees he will one day rule JacMar Corporation.

GUILT, ALIENATION, SUSPICION

It's hard to accept unmerited good fortune, and guilt is rampant among the wealthy. Inheritors may be consciously apologetic or arrogantly contemptuous—both ways of dealing with unrecognized guilt feelings. They need and want a sense of entitlement. (There's that word again.) Especially when he was younger, JJ tended to roll over people, put them down, criticize them in front of others. Looking back, he sees this behavior as masking his own insecurity and guilt at being the boss's son.

Alienation and feelings of separation afflict wealthy people. If born to affluence, it's hard to understand the lives and experiences of people in ordinary financial circumstances. One can socialize with wealthy peers at clubs and in other expensive activities, but there's always a sense of the group being different from most people. Karen, who was born into the affluent life style, is not sensitive to other people's financial situations and seems to assume that everyone has the money to do what she wants to do. Those who hold back (because they can't afford her expensive tastes) seem cold to her. Since her mother never engaged in community service while she was growing up, Karen had no role model nor was she encouraged to volunteer for such work. Her high earnings help her keep up her expensive habits.

There is an old adage: "When a man of wealth meets a man of experience, the man of experience gains wealth and the man of wealth gains experience." It's hard for the wealthy to take human relationships at face value: "What does he or she want from me?" Suspiciousness, even paranoia, are protective coatings. JJ is suspicious of the praise he receives for his community service. Are these accolades genuine? Or are they just to insure that JacMar's charitable contributions will continue?

MEN, WOMEN, AND WEALTH

Men face different problems with wealth than women. Even in this gender-enlightened era, most families favor sons over daughters as successors to the business. JJ and Frank had difficulty with their career choices. Karen moved away from the family to establish her credibility and to escape Jack's chauvinism. Margaret carries a lifelong bitterness for the way she was ignored by her father as his possible successor. Her anger is very real: She is a victim of the "Honey, don't worry your pretty little head" syndrome.

PUT-DOWNS, OPTIONS, AND FEAR

Those not privileged by wealth have a hard time feeling sympathy for the rich, who should be able to afford a constant state of bliss. Frank gets little sympathy when he shares a personal problem with his golf buddies. In their view, someone who can play golf all the time just imagines he has personal problems.

Yet there *are* problems. Excessive options plague the wealthy, and few cope successfully with all the things money can buy. Endless options can paralyze the decision-making process. Frank had the option to drop out into a ready-made job at JacMar. He had the option to adopt golf as his work style. Some say he has it all. But he doesn't have his father's approval. And that gnaws at him terribly.

Fear of losing wealth is prevalent, though seldom conscious. "What would I do if I *had* to support myself? Make my own way? I would panic if I lost my money. I could never survive. I would die!" The "bag lady" syndrome. At times, fear of failure plagues all of us, and some inheritors won't face challenges because they aren't sure they have what it takes to surmount them. Margaret knows these fears. She fought them when Jack first went into business. What if Jack failed? What if they lost what little they had? The same feelings revisited her when Jack had his heart surgery three years ago. "If Jack can't run the company, will we lose everything?" Margaret knows that most of their family wealth is tied up in JacMar Corporation. If her sons replace Jack, can they keep the company profitable? Must she rely on their management to support her in her old age?

Inheritors who succeed on their own still battle the pressures to substitute money for services. It's so much easier to write a check than to do hard work. Moreover, other people want your money more than your accomplishments. This is particularly distressing to inheritors who are involved in charitable work. Does the money they are expected to contribute obscure their personal abilities? This may produce a game where inheritors pretend they aren't wealthy, but work very hard at charitable roles, hoping that their competence will be recognized. JJ spends lots of time in civic work. He has been president of several community organizations. At least *there* he is in charge. At least *there* he is respected for his accomplishments! Or is he? Is he elected president just to keep the JacMar contributions coming? He doesn't know. He can't know. And it troubles him.

PARENTING WEALTHY CHILDREN

Wealthy families can afford personal and domestic help and boarding schools, but these are only second-class surrogates. They can't provide the personal attention and caring that children need from their parents. If parental nurture is faulty or inadequate, it's hard for children to deal with maturity and to become *trusting* adults. Unfortunately, many wealthy parents are busy and active and neglect their children. Margaret was a full-time parent to her sons. After Karen was born, however, Margaret foresaw increasing demands on her time as the company grew, and she hired full-time domestic help, a nanny. Karen will tell you that, in many ways, Nanny was her *real* mother; Margaret always seemed to be away with Jack at some convention or business trip. Although Nanny was kind to Karen, no one could replace her mother. Margaret realizes that now, but the gap between them continues. Margaret calls Karen every day.

It's hard to be part of a dynasty. Parents' expectations can be excessive if the family has an established tradition of wealth and position. Dynastic families rear their children under pressure for high achievement and general excellence, whether personally, socially, or at school. While this works well for some inheritors, it works against others if the same standards are applied to all children regardless of talents, interests, or aptitudes. It's difficult to establish an individual identity while being seen as part of the family dynasty, particularly if your parents are well known.

"Why can't you get good grades like your brother?" Frank was always hearing. "Why are you so messy? See how neat JJ's room looks." His father's words of long ago still hurt. The worst hurt, however, came a year or so before Jack's surgery. The oldest salesman under Frank's supervision was a hopeless alcoholic. All treatments had been tried; all failed. Frank suggested to his father that the failed employee be granted early retirement. Jack exploded, "Frank, you never will understand loyalty, will you!" How these words cut Frank to the bone! He felt sick, rejected. A few weeks later, he was arrested a second time for driving while intoxicated.

Being rich liberates and entraps at the same time. The wealthy are free to do or have what money can buy. They are free from the fear of want, from the agony of not being able to provide for those they love. But the wealthy can also be prisoners of wealth. Wealth can isolate, narrow friendships, create gnawing self-doubt about what they could accomplish if they were up against it. It's a lifelong struggle to be responsibly wealthy. Having wealth is only the beginning of the journey.

RAISING RICH KIDS

All affluent parents are concerned about the effects of "too much too soon." Billionaire businessman Warren Buffet says his children will receive nothing beyond good educations and an emergency fund. Jack and Margaret have drawn the line: Their children must work in order to maintain their life styles. "It's not right to bring them up on steak, then make them switch to hamburger," says Jack. Good child rearing is especially important for wealthy families. Good nurturing requires lots of love, training, counsel; good examples by *both* parents, all the way through childhood, adolescence, and beyond. *Indeed, parenting never ends!*

Parents need to be very good listeners. While there is much emphasis on "quality time," parents also need to be there when nothing seems to be happening. Strong parenting is important for all children, but it is especially important for children who grow up with the paradoxical problems of lifetime financial security and comfort. Affluent parents need to help their children through frustration and disappointments when there is a great temptation to quit. Perhaps Jack was right in insisting that Frank graduate from college.

Surrogates play significant roles. Inheritors often talk about personal and domestic help's crucial roles in their growing up—Karen talks about Nanny that way. Once Margaret told Karen she was going to discharge Nanny for neglect of household duties. Karen was devastated. Karen had friends whose nannies neglected them, were cruel to them. Karen feared her mother would replace Nanny with one of them.

ATTITUDES

Constructive attitudes about wealth begin with parents. Parents need to be comfortable, clear, and balanced about their own wealth—free both of pride and shame about it. Parents who have unresolved problems about wealth need to work through them, lest they contaminate the children. They also need to examine how the way they manage money inevitably teaches their children, for better or for worse. At times Karen thinks her mother "bought her off" with things instead of giving time and attention.

In some families, talking about wealth is as taboo as talking about sex. But remember that a refusal to talk about something suggests that the subject matter is dark and shameful. Some inheritors don't know the origins of the family fortune. Sometimes these origins are cloudy, even scandalous. Try candor here, and invoke the family's resolve to use present wealth responsibly. Jack's children are proud of his business and his accomplishments. Their heritage is clear.

SCHOOLS AND CAREERS

Choosing a school is a very individual decision. Intellectual, psychological, and emotional factors all play important parts. Usually it is wise not to insist that children go to the same schools their parents attended, to actively involve them in the process. For Jack, nothing would do but that all three children attend his alma mater unless they won scholarships to other schools or paid their own expenses. Jack hoped this would encourage his sons to become engineers. Again Margaret intervened and persuaded Jack to let the children choose their own colleges. JJ, though bright, wasn't interested in engineering; Frank dropped out. Surprise: Karen adored her engineering program at Jack's alma mater.

Following father's footsteps can lead one down a blind alley. Work that fulfills is critically important to an inheritor's welfare, so if making money in the family business has become meaningless, a child may be heading for trouble. An inheritor may need to look outside to be fulfilled in the arts or humanities, or in teaching, government, politics, or social work. Frank has found a way to combine his need to work with his love for golf.

FRIENDS

Inheritors need friends who are not out to exploit the relationship. These friends may be wealthy, or just be able to relate to a wealthy friend without flattery or manipulation. JJ and Judy have limited their social circle to financial peers. Frank's friends are largely golfing buddies. Karen wishes she could conceal her wealth from her coworkers and friends, but her tastes and lifestyle choices betray her.

LIFE-STYLE CHOICES

Karen knows she could support herself without the family money. JJ and Frank aren't so sure. As time passes, the brothers feel golden handcuffs binding them tighter to JacMar Corporation. They couldn't duplicate their life styles on "the outside" and they worry they couldn't make it if the company failed.

Support is one thing; spending is another. Margaret can buy almost anything she wants. She enjoys her comfortable life style. Though Jack complains about her overspending, there is always money in her checking account, and he always pays her credit-card bills. Even with two incomes, JJ and Judy live rather modestly—both are savers, investors. Frank is always out of money, and Frances is forever spending what they don't have. Frank has borrowed heavily from JacMar Corporation, which infuriates Jack. JJ and Judy think these loans unfairly favor Frank. Margaret sees no problem since Frank and Frances have four children to raise and Frances doesn't work outside the home. Karen tries to live on her salary, but can't.

Inheritors should choose a life style that fits them and their resources. If they crave luxury (and can afford it) so be it. If they wish to live modestly, they can certainly afford it. Inheritors should avoid a life style dictated by their parents or by what others think of them, and should be free to change their life styles as they grow older.

Inheritors will be the parents of inheritors. JJ and Judy have resolved not to spoil Jack III with too much, too soon. Frank and Frances tell their children they will be rich some day. Karen vows that she will never use money to manipulate her children.

Wealth is neither an unadulterated good nor a catastrophe. Problems do come with it. An awareness of potential problems allows inheritors to live lives that are full, creative, and satisfying; a life in which money can truly enrich the recipients.

Inside Your Business Family . . .

Are there money-related self-esteem problems in your family? Because of the availability of family wealth, do any members suffer from lack of motivation? Lack of self-discipline? Boredom? Guilt? Have any suffered recent put-downs from friends or associates who appear anxious? Is there fear of losing wealth in your family? How do the fearful cope?

Has parenting in your family been affected adversely by wealth? In what respects?

Can your family discuss money comfortably? Or are money discussions awkward, painful, even taboo?

Does your estate plan take into account the impact of wealth on your inheritors' lives? How have you balanced giving to and withholding from your inheritors?

What are your inheritors' wealth expectations from you? Have you talked with your inheritors about their wealth expectations? Do your inheritors know the origins of their family wealth?

How do you handle relationships between your children and

personal and domestic help? To what extent does your wealth limit your social contacts? Your children's social contacts? To what extent are those limitations healthy or unhealthy?

In what respect is your wealth a handicap to family members? What can be done about these handicaps?

What's your family policy on the selection of schools? The selection of friends?

12

RESULTS COUNT!

My father said, "If you expect a job description, you are not going to get it."

—*Katie Ford, Vice President, Ford Models, Inc.*[13]

Critical Question 9: *How should we evaluate and pay family members who work in the business?*

Critical Question 10: *What should be done if a family member doesn't perform or leaves the business?*

There are jokes about family business payrolls, most of which have to do with how many family payrolls are skewed, unrealistic. The most common scenario has some family members overpaid and correspondingly underworked, but some are underpaid but overworked. Both situations can raise problems.

OVERPAYMENT

Overcompensation from the company is an easy, usually tax-efficient way of distributing family largesse. But overcompensation may also reflect guilt feelings. Jack took lots of time away from his family during the years he was building JacMar Corporation, but insists he "did it all for them." Nevertheless,

72

Jack has some guilt feelings about his absence during those important years when the company was his favorite child. Overpaying his sons is a way of salving his conscience as well as a way of keeping the younger generation attached to the family business. Jack may fear the boys could not earn equal pay "on the outside" and so he binds them with golden handcuffs. At ages forty and thirty-eight, though, JJ and Frank are beginning to feel their golden handcuffs pinch.

Overcompensation may also reflect inequity and injustice among members of the younger generation. The ancient Greeks had a rather simple formula for dispensing justice: "Treat all equals equally." In Margaret's view, all of her children are equals, therefore JJ and Frank should be paid exactly the same compensation from the company—and they are. Now, equal compensation for all siblings works fine in some families, even though they make unequal contributions to the business. But consider the Romans' view of justice: "Render to people what each is due; but be prepared to justify the differences." In most family businesses, compensation differs according to the family employee's value, experience, and expertise, even though it may be difficult to justify those differences to the family members who make less. Jack is clearly inconsistent in overpaying his sons then complaining that each is paid more than he is "worth," yet it is his only way of reconciling his mixed emotions.

JOB PERFORMANCE

Complaints about the job performance of family members are common: They aren't getting along with other employees; they come late to work, leave early, sometimes don't come at all. We also hear lots of constructive concerns about the job performance of family members: She's working too hard; she needs some help; he needs more training; he's got a lot to give, but he's in the wrong slot; she needs a vacation.

What is not heard often is feedback about the quality of job performance of family members. Most business families have good job performance review programs for unrelated employees but place family members outside the loop. This is unfortunate, because most of the comments they get from others can be pretty unrealistic.

Much of what JJ hears about his job performance comes from employees who are trying to stay on the good side of his father. As a consequence, JJ is overpraised and undercriticized. What JJ really needs is an arm's-length performance review from a knowledgeable person: Al, JacMar's general manager. But will Al tell JJ what he really thinks about how the heir-apparent is doing his job? Most likely, Al will be candid if Jack supports him. Indeed, at home Al confides to his wife that perhaps JJ could lead the company. "But I don't want to be there," he says. For Al, things would just not be the same without Jack at the helm.

Adverse performance reviews can be bitter medicine. But that medicine keeps family employees healthy. There is no reason to omit family members from regular performance reviews. They need them as much or more than other employees. It can be done, and it should be done.

FIRING OR RETIRING A FAMILY MEMBER

It's a delicate matter to handle a family member who is not performing his or her job. Retaining a nonproductive family member creates serious morale problems among other employees, and it's not fair to the family member to tolerate continued underperformance.

An unproductive family member sets up a collision between family values and business values. Family values teach us to nurture family members, business values tell us to discharge unproductive employees. Why are unproductive family members retained? Certainly not for business reasons. Keeping them on is necessarily a family decision. So, too, is letting them go.

We suggest families form a Family Council to deal with mixed business and family issues (see Chapter 19 for details on setting one up). The Family Council is an appropriate venue in which to review the family reasons why an underperforming family member should or should not be retained.

Inside Your Business Family . . .

Review your family payroll. Who is being overpaid and by how much? Who is being underpaid and by how much? Are these younger generation members of the family?

What would it cost to hire a nonrelative to do each job presently held by a family member?

Where there is overpayment, would the IRS permit your company to deduct the entire compensation as a business expense?

Where there is underpayment, how much could each underpaid family member earn on the outside?

How might you involve younger generation members to resolve compensation disputes in your family?

Do family employees receive regular, written job-performance evaluations? If they do, are these evaluations candid and clear? If they don't currently receive these evaluations, how could your company institute the process?

Has your company ever discharged a family member for unsatisfactory job performance? If so, how was the discharge handled? What was the family told? Could your company do so if the occasion arose?

13

FATHERS, SONS, AND SUCCESSION

He's my son and he can do it!

—An Wang[14]

One of my favorite books about a business family is Charles Kenney's *Riding the Runaway Horse: The Rise and Decline of Wang Laboratories*. Kenney opens his tale with:

> For the space of a dream, the brilliant blue glow of the Wang Laboratories logo seemed to shine from the pinnacle of the American computer industry much as it did from the top of the massive Wang towers in Lowell, Massachusetts. Founded in 1951 by a Chinese immigrant who had only his genius and his name to give to his company, Wang Labs had grown by 1985 into a far-flung empire with revenues approaching $3 billion. A share of Wang stock, purchased on its first day of trading at $12, was worth an astonishing $800 at the company's height. But disaster lurked just around the corner. By 1991, Wang stock had fallen to an all-time low of under $3 and the company's fortunes have plummeted even more precipitously. . . .
>
> An Wang held dear the Confucian teachings on which he had been raised, teachings that all but sanctified the relationship

between father and son. Now, as he neared the end of his life, An Wang was about to do violence to that most sacred of relationships. . . . An Wang's dream had long been to pass on his corporate empire and to have it flourish under the guidance of his two sons. But it was not to be. This dream that had seemed so tantalizingly close had become a nightmare. On this very day An Wang would fire his son.

After immigrating from China to the United States at age twenty-five, An Wang earned a Ph.D. from Harvard. Along with other very bright persons, he worked on the cutting edge of the computer revolution. What set him apart from most of them was his business sense and extraordinary determination.

After a dozen years of moderate success, he developed the Wang calculator and sold them by the truckload. Later, far ahead of the field, he pioneered the Wang Word Processing System. From 1977 to 1982, revenues doubled every other year and his work force exploded from 4,000 to 24,800. So exhilarated was An Wang by his success that he seriously considered placing an ad in the Wall Street Journal predicting that Wang Laboratories would shortly overtake IBM as the nation's top computer company. Only the protests of his top lieutenants deterred him. Although he amassed great wealth, he had little appetite for its trappings (at any given moment, his work attire consisted of one of two identical gray suits). His obsessive desire was to run the company precisely as he wished, then to pass it along to his two sons, Fred and Courtney. And so, in November 1986, Fred was installed as president of Wang Laboratories against the wishes of Wang's outside directors; An Wang simply told them:

"He is my son. He can do it." His father removed him in August 1989.

Fred couldn't. By 1989, the company was on the knife-edge of bankruptcy, and Fred had to take the fall. He became the symbol for what went wrong at Wang Laboratories. When he left, the stock increased 20 percent in value. But Fred was not the only reason for the company's demise. Says Kenney:

When those who knew the company best searched for an explanation, their eyes settled not on Fred Wang, but on the one man who had maintained an iron grip on the company for nearly forty years. These people wondered whether the visionary Dr. Wang may have grown a bit myopic in his later years, whether he had succumbed to the great danger inherent in running a family business—*placing the family's role in the company ahead of the health of the business.* (p. 10. Emphasis added)

His story, and that of his company, contains the essential elements of a classical tragedy. Within the story, there was conflict between the main character and a superior force in the universe. In Wang's case, the superior force was no less than the weight of thousands of years of Chinese tradition. Most important, An Wang was a heroic character whose story ended disastrously not through happenstance, not because outside forces intervened to rain down upon Wang some terrible fate, but because of choices he freely made. It was with good reason that those who knew the company best wondered whether the man who shattered the dream of An Wang was none other than An Wang himself.

Wang *was* the company. Nothing happened without his knowledge, and everything was done precisely the way he wanted it. Although he hired some brilliant associates, he did not delegate effectively. His secretary often heard him repeating over and over, "You should ask me first. You should always ask me first." As the company grew, he did not consciously delegate more, and he didn't realize he simply could not know or control everything.

As is the case of many companies experiencing furious growth, Wang neglected establishing an infrastructure. There was no formal organizational chart, and everyone reported to Dr. Wang. There was a shortage of management controls. Fred Wang advocated products that were IBM compatible, but his father resisted. He wanted Wang to be the standard, and the world to be compatible with Wang. Once IBM began producing software that could duplicate the Wang Word Processing System as well as perform a thousand other tasks, a commentator remarked that the Wang product was like "a tractor that would only bale hay," whereas the IBM personal computer was "a tractor that could bale hay, plow a field, haul timber, and do dozens of other chores as well" (p. 167). When personal computers began to replace word processors, it was the beginning of the end for Wang Laboratories.

The management problem was a serious one, born of the speed and size of the company's growth, in which many of the conventions of business were tossed aside. There were no business plans and few controls. There was no discipline, no middle management, and top-level management was poor. They struck oil with word processing and money poured out of the ground. When the well stopped pumping, there was no foundation on which to build the next product. There was always the mentality that they wanted to hit the home run.

Kenney concludes:

> Perhaps Fred's most serious mistake was taking the job of president in the first place. Fred knew his father better than anyone, and he knew that his father would not permit him to run the company the way he wanted. Although Fred held the title of president, he could do only what pleased his father. . . . He never had full control. He was always second-guessed. Fred had his father's optimism and his fathers sense of invincibility, but he lacked his father's genius (p. 300–301).

Dr. Wang did not make a great many mistakes, but the ones he made were serious and carried long-term ramifications. He permitted, and perhaps encouraged, the creation of that aura of invincibility around himself that fostered a dangerous and ultimately destructive overreliance on him. His presence within the company was so large, and the faith in him so great, that he was the spiritual leader of the place. His aura served as a kind of buffer, keeping out unwanted distractions but also excluding the kind of criticism and dissent that is crucial for the chief executive to hear.

Wang sometimes used the company as his private fiefdom. He permitted both of his sons to work in vaguely described jobs where they did little real work, and ignored anyone who suggested to him that he turn the company over to anyone but his son. Ultimately, he was guilty of hubris. He believed he could solve any problem; that, even if he made a mistake, he would recognize it quickly enough to rectify it. To me, the saddest part of the Wang story is that An Wang was responsible for the damage done to his beloved company and to his beloved son.

Inside Your Business Family . . .

What is new in this story? Perhaps only the trappings: the computer explosion, Chinese origins, publicly held shares, and considerable notoriety. We often encounter families who are tempted to retell this story in their own lives. An Wang may have been blind to his son's inadequacies. Other fathers are blind to the considerable strengths and skills of their sons and daughters.

It's hard for parents to appraise their children's gifts realistically. That's part of our job, and it isn't always easy. Too often, as business family consultants we are asked: "He's my son. Do you think he can do it?" We direct families to experts who counsel heirs-apparent realistically about their interests, aptitudes, and skills—their general fitness to run the family business. This is crucial. Fred might have been adequate presiding over Wang Laboratories as its chairman of the board were there capable nonrelatives in charge of operations; the Wang family would have continued to control the business, even though publicly traded.

14

SUCCESSION

My father was the driving force, but I knew I'd get my chance. It just happened to come sooner than expected, and you never know what you can do until you're in a position to do it.
—*Kenneth J. Feld, CEO and Chairman, Ringling Bros. And Barnum & Bailey Combined Shows, Inc.*[15]

Critical Question 11: *How do we select the next leader of the company?*

Critical Question 12: *When do we decide who will be the next leader of the company?*

Critical Question 13: *When and how should leadership transition take place?*

Critical Question 14: *How do we evaluate our new leader's job performance?*

Critical Question 15: *How do we provide meaningful careers for other family members who are not chosen to lead?*

Agatha Christie, the mystery writer, introduces us to impatient spouses, lovers, or would-be heirs who just can't wait! So they murder the person who stands in their way. We haven't yet run across a family business successor so impatient as to "do the older generation in," at least not physically. But far too many aspiring younger generation members wrestle daily with incredible impatience. Their impatience strangles vital and delicate family relationships. Work is life to Jack. In an emotional sense, planning succession is like planning his funeral. Jack will be *grieving* through the succession process.

ISSUE NUMBER ONE FOR MOST FAMILIES

Dreary statistics claim to support the hazards of succession in business families. It was once thought that only one in three family-owned businesses continues in the family during the second generation after founding. It was further thought that fewer than one in three second-generation businesses continue to be family-owned in the third generation. Although these statistics have been discredited, there is no doubt that succession is difficult for many business families, and that many family-owned businesses are sold or shut down because the family didn't satisfactorily handle the succession issue. The worst-case scenario is when the founder dies suddenly and unexpectedly without any planning for succession. Equally dire is the founder who stays too long after his business judgment has become clouded by age or disease. Or perhaps the founder steps down too soon before his successor is trained or sufficiently experienced in the leadership roles.

Put yourself in the place of JJ, the aspiring CEO of JacMar Corporation. Since childhood, JJ has had mixed feelings about succeeding his father—feelings of anticipation and feelings of dread. JJ is a superb computer scientist but is not an engineer like his father. JJ is academically well trained in management, but lacks his father's charisma.

JJ is worried that if Jack hangs on indefinitely, there may be little left of JacMar Corporation when death or disability forces Jack to give it up.

Father and son have never discussed the details of succession. JJ has never raised the subject with his father, nor has Jack confirmed that JJ is his heir-apparent. JJ operates from day to day on a set of assumptions that are favorable to him, hoping desperately that his assumptions will come true. He doesn't know whether his father shares these assumptions, and no clear career path points his way to future leadership.

Adding to these uncertainties are JJ's inflated corporate title and paycheck. Like so many younger generation members, JJ is forever "being groomed," "learning the business," "warming up in the bullpen." Like Stanley Marcus, whose forty-year-old contemporaries were already heading public companies, JJ envies his own contemporaries who are already rising stars in non family companies. JJ feels his options slipping away daily; were he to leave JacMar Corporation today, his resume wouldn't be very impressive—eighteen years with the family business. He feels "kept," like a prisoner in golden handcuffs.

JJ's life is a succession of frustrating "todays" spent restlessly in the vague hope that some "tomorrow" he will finally achieve his dream—that is, if he *wants* that dream. Perhaps most painful is JJ's realization that his "tomorrow" won't come until after his father is dead. His father shows no signs of retiring or relinquishing control. JJ loves, respects, admires, and fears his father, but does that mean he is doomed to park his manhood until his father dies? Isn't there some way JJ can be fulfilled today?

Karen, too, is having problems with her present and the future. Over the years, her parents have given her company stock, and she has a "paper" net worth of a million dollars. Yet the stock pays no dividends and there are no distributions in excess of her share of tax liability for company profits. Karen and Kenneth want to start their family, but Kenneth needs a year off work to earn his MBA degree. Karen would like to use her JacMar stock for "today" needs. But Karen is afraid of offending her parents if she asks. She doesn't want to sound ungrateful, but the family has never discussed how a child would "cash out" of JacMar Corporation. Like her brother JJ, Karen has always thought of *spendable* money from her JacMar stock as a "tomorrow" thing—money she would have after her parents' deaths.

JJ and Karen have always been sibling rivals, even as adults, competing for the approval of their strong parents. JJ feels that Karen has an unfair advantage as a female, particularly with their father. Karen thinks JJ has an unfair advantage as the oldest son, particularly with their father. She has begun to hint that her brothers may both be overpaid for their services to JacMar Corporation, that they are both receiving an undue portion of family wealth. Karen s hints infuriate JJ: *He's* the one who must suffer the daily frustration and occasional humiliation of being Jack's potential successor, while *she* is getting a free ride. Trouble is building as the "mine, mine, mine . . . eventually" theme emerges. Both JJ and Karen are frustrated *today* by real-life problems that can only be solved (or so they think) by the deaths of their parents. Both feel frustrated. Both feel very guilty.

In some parts of Pakistan, when a business owner dies, his business assets are burned with his remains on the funeral pyre. His children start over again. This custom certainly avoids the kinds of succession problems faced by American business. But burning business assets would also destroy a precious part of the American dream: immortality through the business. This American Dream of business immortality has kept Jack going. He is on the verge of realizing his dream if he and his family can breach the chasm of succession. But to Jack, it's his "todays" that are golden; his "tomorrows" are problematical. At his stage in life, Jack thinks that "Someday this will all be yours" should reassure his children, giving him time to savor his considerable accomplishments.

One of the gravest threats to continuity—successful succession in American family businesses—is the inability to sort out "today" from "tomorrow." The issues that confound JJ and Karen should not be dismissed as hangups of the "Now Generation." The second-generation JacMars are not spoiled kids demanding yachts and shiftless lives. They are adults trying to answer some of life's most basic questions in the context of their successful business family. And the only answer they hear today is that there will be no answers until their parents die.

Unfortunately, for restless younger generation members like JJ and Karen their "todays" and "tomorrows" are out of sync. Working out the solution intergenerationally may produce anger and tears, but it is critical that older and younger generations understand each other's "todays" and "tomorrows" and how each feels about it. Left alone and unattended, "Someday this will all be yours" and "mine, mine, mine . . . eventually" could wreck the business and the family.

SUCCESSION IS A PROCESS

Once the family decides to keep the business, it's time to begin planning for the process of succession. Successful management transition involves much more than selecting a future CEO. Succession is a *whole-family process* that affects everyone in the family deeply and differently: It will change the family system forever. More often than not, the new business leader also becomes the next leader of the family. Jack is the acknowledged leader of the JacMar family, even though his leadership is flawed. If JJ is to succeed his father as CEO, can JJ also succeed as leader of the family?

Jack wants a person with extraordinary talent to succeed him. Doubtful that either son has that talent, Jack has been talking secretly with Nelson, a gifted public company executive who was "downsized" in a recent merger (he hasn't even told Margaret). Margaret insists the successor be one of her children. JJ thinks he's entitled by being the oldest and most responsible son. Frank knows he won't be selected but opposes his brother. Karen doubts that either brother can do the job, but isn't a candidate herself so long as Jack is active in the company. It's doubtful that a family discussion of succession will be productive unless each member can find a way to focus outside these preconceptions.

One way to start the succession process is to adopt an emergency plan. Suppose Jack were seriously disabled for a period of six months—who would step in to run the company? When the JacMar family faced a short-term emergency during Jack's heart surgery, Jack named Al, the general manager, to run things. Most families can talk productively about an emergency plan that contemplates the business leader s return.

Another important preliminary step in the succession process involves objective career evaluation. JacMar Corporation could retain a professional career counselor to administer a battery of tests and to conduct intensive interviews with potential successors, including all the JacMar children. Results would be disclosed only to the person evaluated, unless he or she consented to wider disclosure. Thereafter, the counselor would interview Jack and other key employees to ascertain how the potential successor would actually fit into the organization.

Career evaluation usually is a pleasant experience for the persons evaluated, and all of the JacMar children could benefit. Career evaluation involves learning more about one's interests, aptitudes, and skills. The results may suggest job changes or clarify career paths. JJ will receive an objective assessment of his potential for leadership, free of his father's doubts or his mother's ambitions for him. Frank will discover talents and aptitudes not fully developed by his golf course salesmanship that could point to more important tasks for Frank in JacMar Corporation. Although Karen is frequently evaluated by her employer, she can benefit from the independent approach of an outside consultant. Moreover, if her brother's evaluations are disclosed, and the results reflect significant talent, Karen may lay aside some of her doubts about their potential leadership. Equally important, Karen will feel *included* in the succession process, even though she has no aspirations to lead.

"When" can be almost as important as "how" the next leader is chosen. Succession can take place gradually and orderly, but too often the successor is chosen too late—after the business leader dies or becomes disabled. Instead of a planned phase-in of leadership, the successor takes over in crisis. Jack's heart surgery three years ago served as a wake-up call that the succession process should be underway. Chosen too early, the successor may become restless to lead if the incumbent is reluctant to depart. If JJ is selected as heir-apparent before Jack is ready to turn over real authority to him, a damaging power struggle could ensue. Jack needs to realize he doesn't have to retire in order for succession to take place. Jack may be ready to let JJ run company operations now and in two years have Frank become the primary contact with certain vendors and customers. It may take longer for Jack to turn over personnel and finance to them. When employee loyalty has transferred from Jack to the successor, and the banks contact the successor without calling Jack first, the process of succession is probably complete.

It's critically important for the new leader's performance to be evaluated. Jack could do the performance evaluation, or the family could do it. But neither would do it well. Evaluating the new leader's performance is a primary function of the board of directors (see chapter 15, "Activating Your Board").

GUIDELINES FOR SUCCESSION

Succession issues are a huge concern both to family-owned businesses and public companies. One of the first responsibilities of newly elected public company CEOs is to select and train their successors. Some big company CEOs do succession planning well, others are abysmal failures. There may be a pattern of alternating strong CEOs and weak CEOs, reflecting strong CEOs selecting weaker successors who cannot possibly equal their accomplishments, and weak CEOs selecting strong successors who can get the company moving again.

Some succession practices work well in big companies and family companies alike, some don't. Following are some considerations for family companies.

Timing

If the successor is a family member, choose wisely, and choose early. Give the troops an opportunity to adjust, or bail out—in most cases, they already know anyway. Most everyone at JacMar Corporation expects JJ to succeed his father. JJ talks to key employees about some of his ideas for change, and Al, the JacMar general manager, has told Jack he thinks JJ could run the company. Al and the employees are not particularly enthusiastic about JJ, but they seem resigned to his eventual succession.

The Invisible Organization Chart

Draw the "invisible" organization chart for your successor. Explain to your heir-apparent your character analyses of key employees' power and influence. Both the "invisible" organization chart and the official organization chart will change with successor management. Jack's current invisible organization chart looks like a spider web with Jack in the middle, attuned to every little vibration. Like most successors, JJ will substitute a more classical management pyramid for the spider web, both visible and invisible. A more important issue is what to do with those employees who aren't producing. Though he would like to depart as a hero, it's up to Jack to retire or discharge them before he leaves. These unpleasant tasks shouldn't be passed on to his successor.

Identify the Hidden Influentials

In his autobiography, General Colin Powell reveals that in every organization there is a person who knows where the bodies are buried and how to circumvent inconvenient regulations. "That person will be there after the cockroaches are dead."[16] Be sure the successor knows who these people are; they may not have impressive titles (office managers, researchers, secretaries) but their support is essential. Use your accumulated good will to endorse your successor to them. In JacMar Corporation, the "hidden influentials" may not accept JJ as long as his father is still around. If confused about where the power lies, they will gravitate to where they *think* the power lies. After succession, Jack should dismantle his spy network and reject "end run" appeals from employees who plead with him to overrule JJ. Al's support of JJ will be critical.

The Unwritten Rules

Spell out the unwritten rules, pecking orders, hidden agendas, and accepted norms that add up to corporate culture. Even replacements from within might not have detected these subtleties hidden from most of the staff. Family successors usually operate under the assumption that they are "supposed to know" because they come from the gene pool. Not so. It's hard to deal with what you are supposed to know but don't, so, regardless of how simple it seems, talk about little nuances with your successor. Don't worry about coming across as too elementary. Jack hasn't been a very good teacher—his teaching style is, "Sit here and watch me do this"—and his sons still have much to learn from him. When they don't learn, Jack thinks they aren't paying attention, they think Jack is not trying, and they end up arguing. Al, as mentor, has taught the sons what he could about JacMar Corporation, but Al lacks the breadth and vision that can only come from Jack. The sons need a neutral outsider to help resurrect the teaching process. It is of primary importance that Jack finish teaching his sons about the business.

Rivalry and Competition

Since childhood, JJ and Frank have competed for their father's approval. They don't need any further encouragement to compete. These brothers now need encouragement to *cooperate* with each other and with Jack. The three of them should focus on team building. Expert help may use testing and counseling to find new ways to work together.

Making Changes

Don't make your successor a slave to your policies. Encourage and welcome independent thought and action. It's natural for you to want continuity, and a successor's changes can sting the ego of the predecessor, but be realistic. This is the hardest lesson for most family businesses. Because he has the power and owns the shares, Jack can insist on continuing his ways as the price of turning the business over to his sons. Because they have been held down so long, JJ and Frank may jump at the chance to exercise their new powers to invoke change. This exercise could hurt the company—or save it. Jack and his sons need careful discussion and agreement about their freedom to make changes. Here again, an outside board can be invaluable (see chapter 15).

Lasting Impressions

Share your observations about people, but don't impose them. Acknowledge your biases. Sometimes you can bad-mouth a coworker without realizing it. Accept the possibility that your replacement may build a better rapport with certain key people than you have. When faced with new situations, children tend to react like their parents until they have learned to develop different reactions. More than they realize, JJ and Frank will carry their father's evaluations and prejudices. Jack should encourage them to re-examine his ways of thinking, but it won't be easy for him.

Underpraise

Let your successor's credentials speak for themselves. If you over-praise at the outset, your successor will try to live up to your unrealistic expectations and probably fail, resulting in anger and depression. Skip the exaggerated introductions and let your suc-cessor create his or her own impressions. If your successor has your name, that will be burden enough. Let her set her own goals, bask in his own accomplishments—*earn* the name in the eyes of other employees. Remember An Wang, computer genius and founder of Wang Laboratories; he overpraised his son Fred: "He can do it; he's my son!" Fred didn't. Wang Laboratories went into bankruptcy.

Hard Issues First

Plunge your successor into the deep. Immerse your successor in the harder issues at the beginning, even at the risk of overwhelming her or him. Tune your successor into the toughest challenges up front. This is tough love in action. Far too many would-be successors are protected from the hard issues; they should make the hard choices early. Then stick by the decisions.

Letting Go

Ultimately, there's no way you can ensure the success of your successor. Lay the groundwork, set the timetable, then get out of the way. Easier said than done in family businesses. Jack is still around, still the father, still a stockholder. Jack and Margaret will be financially dependent upon the company for the rest of their lives, and his strong influence will continue even after death. But at some point, Jack must remove the training wheels and watch JacMar Corporation wobble forward with JJ on the seat. It's unlikely that Jack will ever be satisfied with his successors and will be sorely tempted to reinsert himself. Chances are, he will criticize his sons for allowing quality to deteriorate and not treat-ing "his people" right. The successor needs to realize that Jack's *grieving* will take time, that JacMar Corporation will forever be his favorite child.

Inside Your Business Family . . .

What are your plans for management succession? Have these plans been discussed in the family? Have they been endorsed by the family?

If your succession plans are up in the air, is there an heir-apparent? Does the family agree that your heir-apparent is the best choice?

Is the "Someday this will all be yours" signal sent in your family? If so, by whom? If so, to whom? What assumptions about the future does "Someday this will all be yours" generate?

How should your family handle the succession issue? What communication barriers prevent a candid discussion of succession? Where should your family begin? With an emergency plan? With career evaluations for the younger generation?

Has a successor to your present business leader been selected? Has his or her selection been announced to the family? To your employees? To customers, suppliers, and bankers? To the public?

If a successor has not been chosen, when is the earliest and when is the latest that selection should take place? What obstacles are in your way? How will your successor's management style differ from that of your present business leader? How will that difference affect your employees?

Who are the "hidden influentials" in your company? What are the most important "unwritten rules" in your company?

What are the most important things your current business leader must teach his or her successor?

What present policies *must* be continued by your successor? What are the "hard issues" your successor must deal with?

15

ACTIVATING YOUR BOARD

Success is intimidating. It surrounds you. Everyone "yeses" you, and no one tells you what you're doing wrong.
—*Roger King, Chairman, King World Productions, Inc.*[16]

Critical Question 16: *Who should serve on our board of directors? Family members? Employees? Our outside advisors? Others?*

Critical Question 17: *How should our board of directors function?*

Critical Question 18: *What should we expect of our directors?*

Boards of directors are the shareholders' elected representatives. On behalf of the shareholders, directors are supposed to set corporate policy and to review management.

Jack has served on other boards of directors, such as his bank's, and is not at all persuaded his company needs "one of those." Jack thinks most big company boards aren't very good models. He sees how in large corporations outside directors (who are not employees of the corporation) may be selected for "trophy" reasons: because they are rich, famous, or because they are close business associates of the CEO. The CEO may return the favor by serving as director on the boards of close business associates. Too often, outside directors of very large corporations eat the plate management sets.

The boards of small corporations usually consist of shareholders, employees, and an occasional advisor to the corporation—its attorney, CPA, or banker—who are beholden to the dominant shareholders. Boards of small companies seldom meet, and if they do, directors vote and sign as directed by the major shareholders. This is typical of JacMar's present board of directors. Jack's directors know how to vote—they just watch Jack. For too many small companies, board meetings are boring, awkward, and embarrassing. Corporations, large and small, need sophisticated, informed, involved, independent directors who question closely, talk candidly, and vote their best business judgment. JacMar Corporation badly needs active, independent, outside directors like these.

LONELY AT THE TOP

Jack is successful, powerful, influential, and wealthy, but uncomfortably alone as CEO of JacMar Corporation. His employees, lawyers, accountants, consultants—are all eager to please him, to do his bidding. But no one really challenges Jack, disagrees with him, pushes him back—no one except for Margaret, JJ, and Frank. Unfortunately, Jack turns a deaf ear when they disagree or ask uncomfortable questions.

Jack is successful because he has been right when it counted most. Jack has managed to live with his mistakes, but how long will his luck hold? There's always the chance that Jack will make the big mistake that will cost him the company he's spent a lifetime building. Wouldn't it help Jack to have someone wrestle with him about the big decisions—someone he trusts and respects? Outside directors can provide:

- valuable insights gained in other business environments

- new and creative viewpoints of your business

- objectivity and candor

- access to valuable business contacts

- a wealth of business experience

- successful approaches to problem solving

It's time to consider an outside board when the company needs fresh ideas and approaches, when it is ready to make positive changes, and when its problems can't be solved by customary ways of doing things.

ISOLATING THE ISSUES

The leader of a business family knows a special kind of loneliness. Many important business decisions have a direct bearing on the family and are clouded by family concerns.

Jack, and others like him, need clear advice on business issues from people who are unobstructed by family pressures. With outside directors' help in deciding what's best for the business, Jack can view his business solely as a business and better resolve what's best both for the family and the business. It's important to insulate outside directors from family conflict. Embroiling them in family disputes will cause them to lose interest and resign. On the other hand, expect outside directors to point out family work that needs to be done.

Where Is Help?

Suppose JacMar Corporation could have direct access to the advice and expertise it needs most. Suppose these experts were *Jack's peers*—business people who can look Jack in the eye because they, too, are successful like him. Suppose those experts were to meet with Jack regularly, wrestle with him over important issues, take a personal interest in all phases of JacMar Corporation, and be strongly committed to its success and profitability. And suppose their expertise were to cost no more than $10,000 to $20,000 per year. What's the catch? Who *are* these people?

These are the outsiders on JacMar's board of directors, *real* outside directors who are:

- outside the business—not employees

- outside the family—not relatives

- outside Jack's circle of advisors—not his lawyer, accountant, banker, or financial consultant

JacMar Corporation can have an excellent outside board even though outsider directors are in the minority. A minimum of two outside directors can make a family business board of directors more than just a voting machine or a signature society. Only one outsider, however, would be a token and hence ineffective.

If Jack initially rejects the idea of outside directors, he is not alone. Most oppose outsiders at first. They don't want to share secrets or risk being outvoted. But Jack is turned off by his present board of directors. Populated by relatives and employees, JacMar's present board does little more than vote and sign as directed. Such "rubber stamp" boards become a nuisance—necessary evils who formally approve sales of real estate, signatures to bank accounts, and endless amendments to the company retirement plan.

Which Outsiders?

Jack will be surprised and flattered at the high caliber of people who will be honored and pleased to serve as his outside directors. What are JacMar's critical needs? Financial? Planning? Technical? Business contacts?

Jack should look for outside directors with useful experience and expertise in those areas of his company's critical need. All outside directors should be *risk-taking peers* of Jack—peers who have built or managed successful companies. Jack might well consider staggered terms for outside directors—one, two, or three years. Some companies require that outside directors rotate off the active board for at least one year after their terms expire.

One important caveat: Business owners must honestly appraise what constitutes an outsider. Anyone who has a financial interest in the company is not an outsider. Jack's accountant and his lawyer both sit on the JacMar board of directors. They won't vote against him because they need to keep JacMar as a client. Suppliers and customers have impossible conflicts of interest between the welfare of JacMar Corporation and the welfare of their own companies. Investors—who include all outside shareholders, related or not—are torn between the company's welfare and return on their investment.

Keeping Inside Directors

It's difficult to deal with unsophisticated board members who may ask irrelevant questions, or be ignored, or be talked down to by knowledgeable directors. Unqualified board members usually inhibit getting things done as competent directors spend too much time trying to educate them. Of course, if family members, key employees, and outside advisors leave the board, they will need alternate sources of current information about JacMar Corporation.

Most inside directors don't belong on the board, but their departures can be very delicate. For example, it would be a very sensitive situation were Margaret asked to step down from JacMar's board. But Margaret is a special case. Since Margaret owns 41 percent of the JacMar shares, she should be a director, even though she is not sophisticated in business. As trustee under Jack's estate, Margaret may someday control an additional 41 percent of the shares. Participation as a director will keep her connected to the company and provide opportunities for her sophistication to grow.

Since the sons aspire to run the company, they should attend board meetings in some capacity, whether as directors or merely as observers. The sons should witness intense discussion of the most important issues facing JacMar Corporation. They should listen to outside directors test Jack's ideas in discussions conducted in "business talk" rather than "family talk." They should hear their own performance and contributions evaluated, knowing that the outside board will eventually decide if and when either is ready to lead the company. Although more distant from the company, Karen should also be invited to the board if her brothers are directors, or to observe, if the brothers aren't directors.

Though they are insiders and may have useful expertise, in-laws' inclusion on the board can be awkward. An in-law may feel compelled to represent a spouse's personal interests rather than the best interests of the company. Given her fragile marriage to JJ, Judy would not be a good choice as director. Frank's wife Frances lacks business sophistication. Karen's husband, Kenneth's close relationship with Jack might impair his ability to be objective and candid.

A BARGAIN

Outside directors usually receive $500 to $2,000 per quarterly board meeting, plus travel expenses and lesser amounts for committee meetings. Some get an annual retainer to cover meetings of board committees. Outsiders should require that the company indemnify them from any liability they incur. If this indemnity is backed up with director liability insurance, the annual premium should be approximately equal to director compensation for the year. If JacMar Corporation pays its outside directors $16,000 per year and another $16,000 in premiums, the annual cost of the outside board is $32,000. Where could Jack obtain such quality advice for that money? This is a real bargain.

Inside Your Business Family . . .

What needs could be met by qualified outsiders on your board of directors? What special expertise should they possess?

How would your company find good candidates for outside directors? Who are the ideal candidates? How would you approach them?

How would your key employees react to outsiders on your board?

Would you be satisfied to have your outside board select the successor to your present business leader?

Would you be satisfied were your outside board to approve compensation and benefits paid to key employees, including family employees?

Would you be satisfied if your outside board were to make dividend decisions?

16

RECONCILING OUTSIDE AND INSIDE SHAREHOLDERS

Will the vice-president closest to retirement please go out and kick his ass?

—*Marshall Field V, Field Corporations*[17]

Critical Question 19: *Who should own stock in the business?*

Critical Question 20: *Should all children own equally, whether or not they work in the business?*

Critical Question 21: *What dividends or perquisites (perks) should shareholders receive?*

Critical Question 22: *How do we balance the interests of inside family shareholders (who work in the business) with the interests of outside shareholders (who don't work in the business)?*

The Bingham family of Louisville, Kentucky, owned a media empire worth hundreds of millions of dollars. Barry Bingham Jr., grandson of the founder, was CEO. In the mid-1980s, family conflict led by Barry's sister, Sallie, provoked a sale of the company that most other family members, including her aged parents, opposed. Sallie Bingham prompted the sale of the Bingham newspaper empire because she felt her ideas—and 4 percent interest in the companies—were not being accorded sufficient respect. Sallie's parents had given her the stock that she later used as a weapon against them. Had they given her something else of equal value, the newspapers and television station might have remained in the family.

Jack and Margaret have given 5 percent of the JacMar stock to each of their children. Karen already has a larger percentage share than Sallie Bingham.

"PARASITES" VS. "PLUNDERERS"

The Bingham experience is, unfortunately, a not-uncommon one in business families. When gifts of stock are made, future battle lines are drawn. In one camp are the inactive shareholders, outsiders who regard the insiders as plunderers of their legacy. Inactive shareholders view their shares in the family business as poor investments because they are too concentrated, offer too little return, and are subject to too much control by insiders who divulge too little information and pay too little in dividends. In the other camp are the insiders who operate the company and view the outsiders as parasites who are detached investors, uninterested in the growth of the business, too insistent on distributions, too vocal with advice and criticism, too willing to inject family concerns into business decisions. If ignored, these "parasites," will cause trouble. Karen now just hints that JJ and Frank are overpaid, but she would say more if their father no longer ran the company.

Ordinarily, there is no market for outsiders' shares except with other shareholders, who usually don't care to buy. Although Karen is worth a million dollars on paper, her 5 percent interest in JacMar earns her no more than is necessary for her to pay her share of the taxes on the S corporation income.

If Jack and Margaret leave JacMar voting shares equally to their children, how will Karen vote on major issues? If JJ and

Frank disagree, Karen's vote will break the tie. But so long as her brothers agree, her vote seems meaningless.

INTERGENERATIONAL PLANNING

In her own book, *Passion and Prejudice*,[18] Sallie Bingham complains about the lack of communication in her family. She has a point. Too often the older generation does its estate planning in secret. There is no discussion with members of the younger generation, who may be asked to invest the rest of their lives in their inheritance—the family business. The younger generation learns the details only after an elder dies.

Jack and Margaret have done most of their estate planning in secret and have not shared many details with their children. Estate planning without communication can be hazardous. Intergenerational estate planning works best where frank and free discussion takes place between the givers and the receivers. One item both generations should discuss is the potential parasite-plunderer scenario. Parents who feel strongly that the company must be divided equally among the children may learn in dialogue with them that the children don't want it that way. Sallie Bingham might have been perfectly satisfied with other assets, but no one asked her—they just gave her stock. Jack and Margaret own the land, the buildings, and much of the equipment used by JacMar Corporation, which they lease to the company. They might consider leaving these leasehold interests to Karen, offset by more stock to JJ and Frank, although they should bear in mind that the lease agreements will need renegotiating from time to time, which could put Karen in a potentially adverse position to her brothers.

Alternatively, Jack and Margaret might leave other assets to Karen or purchase life insurance for her benefit. The JacMar's estate-planning dilemma is very common to business families whose principal asset is an operating company. The company represents over 90 percent of their net worth: The company *is* their estate.

JJ'S NIGHTMARE

Regardless of how well the family gets along now, don't count on harmony forever. Old rivalries, new in-laws, or something completely unforeseen can trigger a conflict between parasites and plunderers.

JJ had a nightmare that transported him thirty years into the future. The family had done nothing to solve its problems in advance. JacMar Corporation was quite prosperous and diversified. In the thirty years, gross sales had risen from $30 million to $175 million. There were now 1,600 employees—but the company still had no established entry rules for family employment. Jack had appointed Al to succeed him as CEO, but shortly after Jack died, Margaret had decided it was time for JJ to take over. Al was given early retirement.

As sole trustee of Jack's estate, Margaret had controlled JacMar Corporation for the many years she survived her husband. Frank had died in a one-car accident on his way home from the country club; his blood alcohol level far exceeded the minimum for driving while intoxicated. Mentally unable to act as trustee in her later years, Margaret had died in a nursing home. JJ, now seventy, had succeeded her as trustee. Stock in JacMar corporation was now owned as follows:

Karen	$1/_6$
Kenneth, Karen's ex-husband	$1/_6$
Frank Jr.	$1/_{12}$
Ernest	$1/_{12}$
JJ as trustee for Frank's daughters	$1/_6$
JJ	$1/_3$

Frances, Frank's widow, still living and not remarried, had no formal connection with JacMar Corporation. Both of her sons had worked for JacMar since their late teens; neither had gone to college. Frank Jr. was in charge of production and distribution; the younger brother, Ernest, supervised the loading dock and seemed content with his job, having spent most of his adolescent years in and out of drug rehabilitation. Frank Jr., encouraged by Frances, was angry and hostile, blaming both Jack and JJ for his father's fatal alcoholism. Malcolm, the husband of Frances and Frank's daughter Megan, was in charge of operations at JacMar Corporation. He shows much more business promise than either of Frank's sons.

Having abandoned her engineering career after divorcing Kenneth, Karen had worked successfully in advertising on the West Coast. She remarried, gave birth to twin daughters, left advertising, divorced her second husband, and returned to JacMar Corporation. At first Karen had been quite visible in charitable activities, functioning as JacMar Corporation's unofficial social chairman and community representative. Company management had come to recognize Karen's considerable financial and accounting talent. She now functioned as chief financial officer, though without the title, and oversaw the accounting and computer operations. Karen was secretary-treasurer of JacMar and vice-chairman of its board of directors. There were no outside directors on the board.

Kenneth, Karen's first ex-husband was a highly paid executive with a public company. Kenneth had acquired half of Karen's JacMar shares in their divorce settlement and was a member of JacMar's board of directors, where he complained loudly and often that the company's internal organization was primitive. Kenneth is the oldest son of Big Al, the former general manager of JacMar.

Karen, always sympathetic to feminist ideals, had encouraged her twin daughters, now age twenty-five, in their own very aggressive feminism. Each twin had asked JJ for employment: one was an engineer, the other an art history major.

JJ's wife Judy, a senior partner in a small law firm, was nearing mandatory retirement age. Their only child, Jack III, was thirty-eight. Like his father before him, Jack III was letting it be known that he expected to be the next CEO of JacMar Corporation. Jack III had an Ivy League liberal arts degree and was single, intelligent, and arrogant. He had just been laid off by an investment banking house where he had worked since abandoning an MBA program.

The Internal Revenue Service had just completed an audit of the company's returns. Having lost its S Corporation status, JacMar was now an ordinary "C" corporation for tax purposes. The examining agent's report disallowed, as unreasonable compensation, the tax deductions for 25 percent of Jack's salary and 75 percent of Karen's salary. Karen had done very little work for the company in the years under IRS audit, when she was using her office and secretary primarily for community service. The agent had not challenged Frances's sons salaries, but had proposed to assess an unreasonable accumulated earnings tax for the years under examination. During those years, JacMar's dividends had averaged 13 percent of current earnings. During the years under examination, Frank's children had threatened JJ with a lawsuit if dividends were not increased. In order to quiet their complaints, they had received newer and more expensive company cars, country club memberships, and the use of the company hunting camp on opening day of the season. Yet their clamor for increased dividends had continued. All of Frank Jr.'s shares were pledged to the bank as security for a loan made to stave off personal bankruptcy. Given his present financial circumstances and spending habits, it was unlikely that Frank Jr. could ever repay the loan unless JacMar Corporation were sold.

JJ woke with a start, wet with perspiration. Judy noticed he was tossing and moaning. The nightmare was a shattering experience. Unfortunately, nightmares sometimes come true.

FAIR? EQUAL?

Though some nightmares come true, nightmare avoidance in business families involves estate planning in the first generation as the very best way to head off nightmares. This means *early* estate planning, before those annual gifts of voting common stock begin. Even at $20,000 per year gift-tax free, they can add up. Sallie Bingham may have received her stock because her parents' advisors pushed for annual gifts that would help them escape tax. Annual gifts make estate planning sense, but annual gifts of voting common stock in the family business *don't* make sense if they create the potential parasite-plunderer situation. If you can, give something else to the children who won't be working in the business.

USING OTHER ASSETS

If, like most family business owners, your assets are predominantly locked up in the company, one way you can create additional wealth is by investing in one of several breeds of life insurance. It makes good *tax* sense for Jack and Margaret to give $20,000 per year to each of their children. Jack and Margaret could give JJ and Frank each $20,000 more in JacMar voting stock, and $20,000 in non-voting stock to Karen. But non-voting shares for inactive children, like Karen, can just rub salt in the wound by depriving them of a voice in company affairs. Shareholders who can't vote are at the mercy of those who can. Instead, life insurance on Jack and Margaret's lives could be purchased naming Karen (or a trust for her) as owner and beneficiary, and part of the premium paid with $20,000 cash gifts to her each year.

YOUR OUTSIDE BOARD

Unfortunately, most parents don't take the foregoing advice and have already given equal shares of voting common stock to active and inactive children alike. What then? This is where your outside board of directors is pivotal. Outside directors must represent *all* shareholders, not just active and inactive family members. Their job is to exercise their best judgment for the benefit of the company as a whole, to create a corporate culture of *accountability*. Their impartiality should regulate the flow of perquisites and dividends and keep the lid on parasite-plunderer conflict—reason enough to justify the outside board's existence. Suppose that, after Jack and Margaret step down, JacMar's board of directors consists of the three children plus two outsiders. So long as JJ, Frank, and Karen agree, they control the board. If one of the children disagrees, they must convince the other two of the outside directors to vote with them.

FOSTERING COMMUNICATION

If shareholders balk at an outside board, there are some tactics that can effect expanded communications among them:

- Circulate company financial information on a regular basis.

- Make annual shareholder meetings informative as well as cordial.

- Keep outsiders abreast of what is happening in the company.

- Call regular family meetings to discuss the business.

PERKS WON'T WORK

If company hunting camps, aircraft, apartments, and the like are available, make sure that all shareholders have fair access. Don't try to buy peace with your parasites by giving them perks such as cars, club memberships, and fringe benefits—most times these just give them something else to argue about.

MORE COMMUNICATION

By all means, *keep direct communications flowing*. Discuss ways of buying out inactive shareholders, and keep that topic of conversation alive. Negotiate if you can. Get everyone to understand that sooner or later the parasite-plunderer tensions could destroy the business. Keep your lawyer, accountant, and other advisors abreast of your discussions, but weigh carefully the consequences of asking your lawyer to speak for you to other family members. Smart business families communicate *directly* with each other, not through third persons. Once families start communicating through lawyers, the risks of family war escalate dramatically. Of course, if there is serious talk of buying or selling, you will want your lawyer present for technical advice and negotiating skills.

Inside Your Business Family . . .

Are there *present* or *potential* parasite-plunderer tensions in your family business?

Do present estate plans give shares in the business equally to younger generation members, whether or not they work in the business? If all shares in your company were left to children who work in the business, are there other assets of equal value that could be left to other children?

Are you presently using company perks to satisfy (or pacify) outside shareholders?

How does Murphy's Law apply to the JacMar Corporation in JJ's nightmare?

As you follow JJ's nightmare:

- How did Margaret use her voting control?

- How will voting control shift when Frank's daughters reach age forty?

- What might have prevented Kenneth's stock ownership?

- How is JJ to handle the requests for jobs by Karen's twin daughters?

- How should JJ handle his own son's request for a job? How will Jack III get along with Frank's sons and his son-in-law?

- When Frank's sons learn of the IRS agent's report, how might they use it against JJ?

- How might Frank Jr.'s personal financial situation cause him to behave toward JJ and the company?

- What might have been done to prevent all of the above nightmares?

17

BUYING OUT FAMILY SHAREHOLDERS

No individual member of the Kiplinger family owns more than 10 percent of this company.
—*Knight A. Kiplinger, Executive Vice President, The Kiplinger Washington Editors Inc.* [18]

Critical Question 23: *What do we do if a family shareholder wants to sell out?*

For some families, a buyout is unthinkable, undiscussable. For most families, a buyout needs intergenerational discussion. These days, Karen is thinking:

Why should I invest my inheritance in JacMar Corporation? Why should my brothers manage my inheritance for the indefinite future? Why should I remain a minority stockholder? My vote wouldn't count, except to break ties between my brothers. Why shouldn't I be allowed to sell some of my stock? This would allow me time to have a baby, take off a year, and pay for Kenneth's MBA program. As a matter of fact, why shouldn't I get out altogether?

Karen has a point. Why should she have her inheritance forever invested in JacMar Corporation and not be able to diversify

her portfolio? Why should her inheritance be managed indefinitely by her brothers, who may not be wise managers? If she is
wealthy on paper, why shouldn't she have some of it to spend
now? Karen has real trouble raising these questions for fear of
misinterpretation. How would Jack take her interest in selling?
As ingratitude? As disloyalty to the family? How would her
brothers take it? As her lack of faith in their abilities? As the
Prodigal Daughter who lacks the decency to wait for her parents'
funerals?

Strangely enough, most families don't think of stock in the
family business as "fungible"—as assets that can be sold or
traded for something of equal value. They think of family shares
as heritage, as a birthright and that to divest one's shares is somehow disloyal. Buying out a family member can be a very delicate
process; if nothing else, it's very awkward to negotiate a price
with other members of your family.

BUY-SELL AGREEMENTS

Many business families sign buy-sell agreements, which give a
family member a "call" (option to buy) or a "put" (option to sell
—either to the company or to other shareholders) on another's
shares. One of the objectives of a buy-sell agreement is to keep
the shares in the family; another *has been* to fix the value of the
shares for tax purposes. In the past, buy-sell agreements have
been heavily tax driven, but the Internal Revenue Code now
imposes transfer taxes on stock at its "fair market value." Broadly
defined, "fair market value" is the price that a willing buyer and a
willing seller would agree upon, each being fully informed, and
neither being under any compulsion to buy or sell.

In a real sense, a buy-sell agreement defines the market for the
shares, even though the "market" is limited to the persons who
sign the agreement. The price or pricing formula dictates the
stock's "value" in that limited market. In a real sense, the buy-
sell agreement price is the value of the shares, because the other
shareholders can "call" them at that price.

Tax-driven buy-sell agreements didn't really contemplate a sale of shares at the death of a shareholder. Most times, there was no "put" or "call," no actual sale of the decedent's shares; the shares simply passed by inheritance. Since the shares were worth no more than the price stated in the buy-sell agreement, who was to complain? No one, except the IRS. In 1985, JacMar's lawyers proposed a buy-sell agreement with an artificially low pricing formula whose purpose was to save estate taxes on the death of Jack or Margaret. Karen refused to sign it. She wanted a fair price for her shares and wouldn't agree in advance to a low buyout price. In 1986, Congress amended the Internal Revenue Code to attack tax-driven buy-sell agreements in order to disallow valuation of stock based on artificially low pricing formulas in buy-sell agreements. The new code provision is designed to force taxpayers to adopt appraised value in buy-sell agreements, but has generated much confusion among tax experts.

DISCOUNTS

Under her parents' current estate plans, Karen would always be a minority shareholder, never owning more than $33^1/_3$ percent. Only if JacMar Corporation were sold would Karen ever receive "full price" for her shares. If Karen's minority shares alone were appraised, the appraiser would discount them, both because selling Karen's shares would not deliver control of the company to the buyer (*"minority discount"*) and further because it would be difficult, if not impossible, to find a buyer for her minority shares (*"marketability discount"*). The combined effect of the minority marketability discounts could reduce the "fair market value" of Karen's shares from 20 percent to as much as 50 percent below what she would receive if the entire company were sold.

Understandably, minority shareholders are usually reluctant to accept such heavy discounts. Sometimes family buyers and family sellers negotiate a higher price that reduces these discounts so that the selling family member receives a price somewhere between the appraiser's discounted value and the price the

shares would bring if the entire company were sold. But if a compromise price isn't reached, and especially if the family is conflicted, minority shareholders may try to provoke a sale of the
company. Apparently this was what happened to the Binghams.
Sallie Bingham was a "parasite" who became so offended at being
excluded from the family business that she provoked the sale of
the entire media empire. Recall that Sallie never owned more
than 4 percent of the shares, and she would never own more
than 14 percent after her parents' deaths.

TAGALONGS

Family buyouts happen. If handled early and fairly, they need not
impair family relationships. But beware: Buyouts are always delicate and almost always emotional. Be prepared for family sellers
to become suspicious. Most of us became "word warriors" as we
grew up in families, wielding infuriating names like weapons in
our attack and our defense against our brothers and sisters. We
still remember those names that would send them into instant
fury. Childish names, childish feelings, childish perceptions.

Here's one of those old warring words with some new meaning: "tagalong." Remember how younger brothers and sisters
would follow us around, and how we made a game of trying to
elude them? They were "tagalongs." Remember how they would
cry because they wanted so desperately to be included in our fun?

Grownup brothers and sisters play a much more serious version of this game when they buy and sell shares in the family
business. In most of these transactions, outsiders (parasites) are
selling to insiders (plunderers). A "low-ball" price buried in a
buy-sell agreement may not be acceptable. (It wasn't acceptable
to Karen.) Families may endure appraisals and exhausting negotiations in order to arrive at an acceptable price. Even so, selling
outsiders can't be sure that the insiders won't sell the company
later on for a much higher price, then pocket the difference.

Enter the "tagalong" agreement. Simply put, a tagalong clause
says that if the purchasing shareholders resell the stock within a

given period of time, the original sellers will participate in the profit as though they had kept their shares. Here's how a tagalong works.

Suppose JJ and Frank were to buy out Karen's 2,000 shares for $500 per share, total $1 million, with the sale subject to a tagalong clause for the next five years. Three years later, JJ and Frank sell the company for $1,000 per share, twice as much as they paid sister Karen. With a tagalong agreement, Karen would receive another $1 million from the proceeds of the sale of JacMar.

Perhaps the brothers had no intention to sell JacMar Corporation at the time they bought out Karen, and had no idea at the time they would receive such a large offer. But could they ever convince Karen? A tagalong agreement costs them nothing and buys them considerable freedom from Karen's suspicions. If a resale becomes irresistible, the tagalong imposes fairness.

On the other hand, if the business sours and JJ and Frank eventually sell at a price lower than they paid Karen—well, that's free enterprise. And Karen will probably trust them forever.

Inside Your Business Family . . .

Are Karen's apprehensions reasonable? Why shouldn't the family buy her out? Does your family business have a buy-sell agreement? If so, do you know how it works and how the price is calculated? Would the pricing formula be *fair* both to a buyer and seller in the family?

Has your buy-sell agreement been reviewed by your tax advisor since 1986? If not, it may be out of date.

Does your buy-sell agreement cover such eventualities as shareholder disability, bankruptcy, or divorce?

Does your buy-sell agreement contain a "tagalong" clause?

18

UNDERSTANDING NEEDS

We don't pay much attention to quarterly results except to see
how we're doing against the budget. Never are we looking for a
quick buck.

—*Howard Cooley, President, Jockey International, Inc.*[19]

Needs make things happen among human beings. We work, play,
love, fight, rest, eat, sleep, dream, dread—because of our needs.
We go into business because of our needs for money, ambition,
aspirations, something to prove. We live in families because we
have emotional needs that can't be satisfied elsewhere.

Business families grapple with a complex mixture of business
and personal needs. Let's begin with the needs of the business.

BUSINESS NEEDS

"The golden goose must continue to lay," as our colleague Ralph
Brumley is fond of saying. "Neglect the golden goose and there
won't be a family business to worry about." Basic needs of the
business include:

- *meeting customer needs through marketing, selling products and*
  services, and maintaining and improving customer relation-

ships. JacMar Corporation enjoys good customer relations thanks to Jack's reputation, his stable of technical experts, and Frank's sales management. But market share isn't increasing.

- *anticipating rapid changes in customers and customer needs— new markets, new products, new competition, new technologies.* In the past, innovation was JacMar Corporations's strong suit. Jack was ferocious about staying out front. Jack's energy is waning, as is his willingness to risk. Waning also is his obsession to stay on the cutting edge.

- *research and development and reinvestment in growth areas.* JJ noted that, for the first time, depreciation was greater than R&D expense last year.

- *profitability—budgeting, control of operating and overhead costs; strategic financial planning; efficient deployment of human and technical resources.* So long as sales increased each year, Jack saw little need for extensive financial planning. But flat sales over the past five years plus more distributions and perks to the family have rekindled his interest.

- *maintaining employee competence and loyalty though hiring, training, career development, reasonable benefits.* Classic employee morale studies confirm that a sense of accomplishment is the most important morale factor. The next most important morale factor is recognition for employee accomplishment. JacMar's key employees are fiercely and personally loyal to Jack. But can this loyalty be transferred to Jack's successor?

- *paying and receiving reasonable compensation, dividends, distributions, and perquisites to family shareholders.* Like most family businesses, JacMar Corporation compensates key employees on the high side and pays generous bonuses to family members in profitable years. Benefit plans are comprehensive and include all family members whether or not they are employees. The company airplane and hunting camp are used to entertain customers and are available to family members. The company pays family dues to the country club and furnishes each with an unlimited gasoline credit card.

- *developing future leadership.* JacMar does a good job developing leadership in middle-management levels. However, future family leadership is in considerable doubt. As to when Jack will retire, and who will succeed him, the company rumor mill is buzzing.

- *developing, redeveloping, and nurturing a business organization that acknowledges, incorporates, and meets the business needs in the list above, and that respects and supports the personal needs in the list below.* JacMar Corporation has an organization chart, but it doesn't actually reflect the way the company really functions. Neither Jack, his sons, nor his senior management are focused on organizational needs or where the organization is going.

PERSONAL NEEDS

Employees look to the company to meet a variety of important personal needs, including:

- *The need for work that provides creative expression and a sense of shared accomplishment with peers, superiors, and subordinates.* JacMar's technicians and engineers work in a creative environment. JJ feels held back and frustrated.

- *The need for work relationships that are caring, accepting, affirming, encouraging, understanding, protective, consistent, and reliable.* Camaraderie among the technicians is high; JJ feels isolated. Frank's country club office is physically remote from JacMar headquarters, but he works hard at maintaining good relationships with his sales force. Jack is in the habit of giving good "strokes" to key employees— but not to his sons. JacMar has a human resources director, but her principal concern is compliance with myriad employment regulations.

- *The need for the opportunity to develop one's knowledge, gifts, and skills to their outer limits.* Technical training is a high priority at JacMar corporation, but there's no formal training program to develop management skills.

- *The need for fair compensation and reasonable benefits, along with an understanding of money, its meaning, its potential, its limits, what is involved in making, spending, and saving money; the relationship of money and self-esteem.* JacMar's compensation philosophy is quite paternal. Fringe benefits are viewed as safety nets against poor money management. It's assumed that employees work for money. How they spend their money is none of JacMar's business.

- *The need to feel like a participant in a value system that defines one's place in the world and gives meaning, purpose, and direction to life.* It's crystal clear that JacMar's highest value is the work ethic. Employees are expected to report on time, to work hard, and to give their all. One's place in the company world is defined by one's willingness to give maximum effort. Overtime is encouraged, vacations are short, child care is provided. JacMar is "like a family"—a very hard-working family. JJ's time away for community service is out of step with company culture.

- *The need for a platform to make a constructive difference in the world.* JacMar employees always give their "fair share" to the local United Way campaign. Although the company encourages civic and community service, time off from work for these activities is discouraged. JJ's extensive civic activities reflect well on the company, but collide with its work-ethic culture.

- *The need for fun, relaxation, and relief from stress and anxiety.* Bowling and softball trophies are on display, but they are several years old. JacMar sponsors an annual company picnic. Excellent meals are served in the company cafeteria, but lunch breaks are limited to thirty minutes. Jack has lunch at a large table in the cafeteria and always eats with

Al, but any company employee is welcome to join them. Most of the luncheon conversation involves business.

OVERLAPPING NEEDS

Fundamental business and personal needs permeate every enterprise. Each company responds to these needs in its own way, according to its own priorities. Large public companies, preoccupied with shareholder pressure for short-term profitability, must focus on their quarterly earnings. Free of pressure from public shareholders, family companies can take a longer view of profitability—go for growth over a decade or a generation. In pursuit of short-term profits, large public companies "downsize" their staffs, notwithstanding the hardship on employees discharged or the increased job anxiety of employees who remain. Without pressure for short-term profits, family companies are freer to retain employees during lean economic times.

Large company managements view their organizations like a computer game—just point and click—whose underlying assumption is that the real emotional underpinnings of employee "loyalty" are greed (for money) and fear (of unemployment). Most family companies view their business organizations as living human organisms, built on fairness to customers and the emotional loyalty of their employees. The family-owned business is usually permeated with family ideals and values. "Our business is like a family."

Take a look at Herb Kelleher, CEO of Southwest Airlines, who goes to great lengths to make his employees' work fun. Southwest Airlines is the fastest growing regional airline in the United States, and by far the most profitable per passenger mile. Kelleher's "work hard and have fun" attitude resonates throughout the organization. Contrary to most public company CEOs, Kelleher understands that his organization is not a computer game but a human organism where complex business and personal needs must be met. In its niche, Southwest Airlines is one of the strongest competitors in the marketplace. In a recent television interview, a Southwest Airlines employee acknowledged, "Yes, work is fun; it's *home* that's work."

REVERBERATIONS FROM THE OWNING FAMILY

By their very nature, family businesses bring their home into work—the company resonates with the relationships in the owning family. This is particularly telling at the key employee level where family intimacy and business leadership overlap most closely. If the owners' family relationship is strong, the operative family virtues of family trust, love, and loyalty have a profound effect on key employees and this permeates the entire business organization. Businesses owned by strong families who lend their strength to the organization are the strongest competitors in the marketplace.

On the darker side, owner family relationships that are distant, cold, or conflictual likewise resonate to key employees and throughout the business organization. If, like the Southwest Airlines employee, "home is work" and work at the office or plant is made more difficult by conflict in the owning family, employees bear a double burden: their own stuff, and the owning family's stuff. *One of the greatest contribution business families can make to their organizations is to get their family stuff together*!

NEEDS AT JACMAR CORPORATION

Despite tensions in the JacMar family, morale at JacMar corporation is quite high and employee turnover low. If not always fun, JacMar is an *exciting* place to work, and there is a waiting list of highly qualified applicants. JacMar is proud of its quality certifications by international organizations. All things considered, a career at JacMar Corporations is about as good as it gets. In an unguarded moment, Jack once said of his employees, "These are my best friends!" Deep inside, Jack is fiercely loyal to his employee-friends: He demands the best from them;

he wants the best for them. They have risked their family's welfare to make him wealthy. Deep inside, Jack wants to protect them from his sons' inexperience and immaturity. Jack's recent heart surgery heightened his employees' anxiety about tomorrow.

THE GOLDEN GOOSE

Business needs and personal needs seldom offset each other. Either they reinforce each other, or else they conflict. If business and personal needs mostly reinforce each other, chances are that both the business organization and family relationships are healthy. In great business families, needs reinforcement is strong despite differences. The golden goose keeps growing and keeps laying. Strong families devote high-energy time to the family, not just leftover time: They structure their life styles in order to enhance the family and work at finding time to be together. They reject the notion that business appointments are sacred but family appointments are negotiable and always subject to being upset. The commitment to family overrides all other commitments in strong families. But this doesn't mean that they are enmeshed. Instead, strong families support the individuation of each member, constantly search for a balance between intimacy and autonomy. Strong families share responsibility, but allow other family members to suffer the consequences of irresponsibility.

SIGNS OF STRONG FAMILIES

Strong families give and receive appreciation, both verbally and nonverbally. Affirming a family member builds self-esteem, and the best way to affirm another person is to *listen*. This means *active* listening—"laying on of ears"—in ways that encourage others to keep talking. Strong families teach respect for individual differences both inside and outside the family, respect for privacy and personal property, respect for cultural diversity. Strong families communicate directly, not through rumor. Strong families don't emphasize competition—competition and conflict are present anyway and don't need to be pushed.

Strong families accept problems as a normal part of life. They try their best to be flexible and adaptable and remain free to change the rules if the situation demands it. They recognize that traditions, such as family vacations and shared holidays, must change in order for the family to grow and mature. Growth is planned for in strong families.

Strong families experience fewer emergencies than other families. Strong families cope regularly with daily irritations because they realize it's the little things that tear marriages and families apart—or more precisely, it's the accumulation of little things.

MURPHY'S LAW IN TROUBLED FAMILIES

In seriously troubled business families, the conflict generated by unmet personal needs and unmet business needs is so strong that the company becomes a battleground. The golden goose becomes the first casualty. Yet too many other family companies teeter in the uneasy middle: Sometimes there is needs reinforcement; sometimes there is conflict; but neither predominates. The golden goose just sits there, treading water.

A business family must sort out the needs of the business and the personal needs of its individual members, or else risk running afoul of Murphy's Law, which holds: "Whatever *can* go wrong, *will* go wrong, and at the most inopportune time." Murphy's law applies *in spades* to business families.

Great business families know to call for help in order to fine tune business needs and personal needs. For them, the business helps to hold the family together as a family and to sustain them as individuals. They're not going to let Murphy's Law catch them.

Seriously troubled business families call for help in desperation, always in deep trouble. This is critical care, damage control. Murphy has already struck.

Business families in the uneasy zone feel the ground shake. Murphy must be on his way. In many ways Jack and JacMar Corporation have stayed a step ahead of Murphy, but when Jack had his bypass operation three years ago, the employees felt the ground shake. Was Murphy on his way?

Inside Your Business Family . . .

In order of priority, list the five most important needs of your business. In order of priority, list the five most important needs of your family. In order of priority, list your own five most important personal needs.

To what extent do unmet needs create conflict in your family? How should these unmet needs be addressed? Where is the best place to start? Do your business needs and family needs reinforce each other? If so, how? Do your business needs and family needs conflict? If so, how?

Are there signs that Murphy be on his way to pay a visit to your business family? If so, what are these signs?

Are business appointments sacred in your family? Do family appointments get pushed aside by business appointments?

How does your family handle irresponsible conduct by family members? Do you cover for them? Do you pretend the conduct didn't happen?

Are your family members good listeners? Does every family member have someone in the family to talk to about personal feelings?

Does your family encourage competition among family members? Do they need encouragement to compete? Do family members compete to please your business leader? If so, how?

How does your family handle emergencies?

Would you classify your family as a strong family? If so, why? If not, why not? If not, what can your family do to become stronger?

19

FAMILY COUNCILS AND FAMILY DECISIONS

> It is an unwritten policy of the Brown family that "We take care of the sons; the sons-in-law are on their own."
> —*Official History George Gavin Brown Family; Brown-Forman*[20]

Critical Question 24: *How do we deal with family disagreements? (Between individuals? Between members of the same or different generations?)*

Critical Question 25: *How do we teach in-laws and younger family members about the values and traditions of our business and our family?*

Critical Question 26: *Who will lead family activities in the next generation?*

Critical Question 27: *How do we help family members who are in financial distress?*

Critical Question 28: *What other responsibilities do we have toward family members?*

Critical Question 29: *What do we do if there is a divorce in the family?*

Critical Question 30: *What if a family member breaks the law or is seriously irresponsible?*

Critical Question 31: *How do we support family members in their own business ventures?*

The Critical Questions help define the work a business family must do. Successful family work begins with a *forum* where family members can:

- express themselves safely

- secure a respectful hearing

- listen to others openly

- discuss constructively

- decide thoughtfully

We support that which we create. A family council encourages family members to make family work their own.

Jack is the dominant member of the JacMar family. It's hard to argue with Jack's success—and it's hard to argue with Jack. Jack is accustomed to command and obedience, he is very quick, and he is practiced at defending his views. Jack's unique perspective of reality is a "given" at JacMar Corporation.

By force of habit, Jack carries his dominant persona into family settings, but when he tries to command he gets resistance. Jack's view of reality isn't shared inside the family and his answers to the 39 Critical Questions—JacMar's family work— might not be accepted by other members of the family. Instinctively, Jack looks outside the family, to "experts," to support his answers.

How convenient it would be if outside advisors could tell the JacMars how to do their family work. Or better yet, how convenient if advisors could do it for them. But outsiders aren't family, aren't members of the gene pool, don't share the family history. *Family work must be done by the family—it can't be delegated.* To do its work, the family must be able to talk together creatively.

For many families, business discussions are difficult and

unpleasant, but families can learn how to talk with each other. A family needs *a process* for settling its differences, it needs to harness its formidable organizational resources to help the family. The beginning of family organization is a family council, which usually begins with a retreat.

ORGANIZING A RETREAT

1. *Get away.* A retreat is just that. Don't hold family retreats at the office or in someone's home. Select a neutral site that isn't loaded with mixed memories. A modest resort can be quite satisfactory, or, if the family has a vacation home that triggers good memories, consider that. JacMar Corporation's hunting camp wouldn't be a good retreat site, because women have never been invited to this location.

2. *Set aside a long weekend.* Arrive on Friday evening, have dinner together, and just be a family. Have fun; socialize. Start fast with work on Saturday morning. Devote no more than six hours to meetings, and leave the rest of Saturday for fun, sports, schmoozing. Set your target to finish by noon on Sunday, but agree that everyone in the family will leave with tasks assigned to do. The JacMars are inviting the third generation.

3. *Consider a facilitator.* Families instinctively shy away from sensitive topics, pretend they don't exist, talk around them. Some important topics involve the consequences of death or disability, some require frank discussions of money and wealth, some are laden with emotion or past hurts. There's a "somebody done somebody wrong song" as background music.

Outside facilitators can help create the agenda, get the family talking, guide the discussion, defuse arguments if they arise. *Don't be afraid of differences!* They will arise, and they may be painful, but you can work through them. The real danger to your family is *silence*—pretending everything is okay and will always be okay. It may not be wise to utilize one of your outside advisors to facilitate your meetings; they may be too close to the family or may become distracted by their own agendas for the family. The best facilitator may have had no prior contact with the family. The JacMar's accountant was invited to facilitate but begged off; he is averse to conflict. Their lawyer volunteered to facilitate but was not invited; he is openly partial to Jack. For the first few meetings, Karen's husband Kenneth was pressed into service. More recently, family members are taking turns presiding.

4. *Update the family.* Most shareholders' meetings are dull and boring, with too much attention paid to just financial information. Family members not involved in the business want to hear about *operations*—about the neat stuff that's going on at the plant, office, or out in the field. Family retreats offer excellent opportunities to do some business education as well as to update what's going on in the family, to hold new babies, get to know new spouses. Perhaps there is new information about family genealogy. Circulate a scrapbook about the history of the business. Margaret and Frances are assembling old photographs of JacMar employees and some of the original corporate documents.

5. *Use the 39 Critical Questions.* At the first retreat it's easier to discuss the importance of each question than to search for answers. See suggestions in the earlier chapter covering the questions.

6. *Assign work.* At the close of the retreat, each family member should have a task to do and a deadline to complete it. Each should clearly understand "who does what, and by when." Here are some sample tasks:

- Consider adding outsiders to the board of directors.

- Improve communications about business operations.

- Draft entry rules for family employees.

7. *Use volunteers.* After the family adopts its list of tasks, ask each member what he or she would like to work on. Try to match family members to the tasks they select. Assign a project and deadline to each task force. Mix older and younger generations members, and include in-laws. Karen's husband Kenneth is eager to help.

All the JacMars are positive about adding outsiders to their board, though Jack is still reluctant to share sensitive information with outsiders, apprehensive about being second-guessed. The JacMars have appointed two committees of the family, one to search for suitable candidates and the other to forecast the effects of outsiders on the board.

8. *Plan the next retreat before you adjourn.* Perhaps your family will retreat once per year and hold its annual meeting as part of the retreat. Other families meet more often, depending on the family agenda. It's important to set a pattern. For large families, particularly those who own larger, older businesses, the family retreat is the only family reunion. And why not? Why not celebrate the privileged life that all share, made possible by the family business? Frank and Frances suggested Hawaii as the site of the next retreat, with the company paying all family travel expenses. After some sensitive discussions, the family adopted a less ambitious budget for its retreats that would not accommodate a Hawaii meeting. Though disappointed, Frank and Frances are reconciled that they received a fair hearing.

9. *What happens next?* After the first retreat, some families hold back, drift away, let those good resolutions made at the retreat take a back seat to more immediate concerns. Some families jump into the work. Like any group, a family needs *organizing,* and for a family in business, organization is critical. Good family organization is a good indicator that the business will survive in the family; the lack of it is a good indicator that it might not survive.

First-generation family businesses might slip by without

organizing themselves, but a good family organization is a *must* for second and third generations if the business is to survive. For inherited businesses, it is particularly important that younger generation members get organized. There's an old Arab saying:

> Me and my brothers against my cousins.
> Me and my cousins against the world!

Continuing an older inherited business requires organizing the common interests of siblings *and* cousins, for the sake of the business and the family. For second and third generations, the annual retreat may become their *primary* family contact. Don't be surprised if your annual family retreat includes the company's annual shareholders' meeting and also doubles as a family re-union. Combining the best of the business and the best of the family relationship in an organized manner is an excellent way to mesh family solidarity with the soundness of the business. Though in first-generation ownership, the JacMars are setting important patterns and attitudes. Jack's crusty demeanor softens around his grandchildren, and the grandchildren are learning that business meetings can be fun.

A SAMPLE FIRST AGENDA

1. Begin with a brief history of the family to remind the larger family of its roots. Display pictures of relatives or important family heirlooms to help heighten the sense of family heritage and solidarity and to educate the children or spouses. Retracing family origins should create a positive atmosphere at the beginning. Include a capsule of family highlights from the past year.

2. Review the history of the business from its origins. This provides an excellent opportunity to share recollections that some of the family members haven't heard. It is also a good opportunity to remind the assembled family of the values upon which the business has been conducted.

Display photographs, scrapbooks, mementos, and important documents.

3. Brief the family on the present status of the company. This would include a general review of operations, research, personnel, facilities and equipment, finances, tax status, etc. Prepare simplified charts and graphs for the benefit of those not tuned in to financial statements.

4. Review current stock ownership. Review any concrete plans for transfer of stock.

5. Brief the family on the future prospects of the business, including the impact of technology, competition, etc. Discuss how the company plans to position itself to remain dominant in this area and any general plans for expansion or change.

6. Go over any concrete plans for internal reorganization of the traditional business, concentrating on the career paths of family members. This assumes that each family member affected has been thoroughly briefed and is comfortable with his or her proposed role in the company.

7. Introduce the family, whether in person or not, to its principal outside advisors, its attorneys, accountants, consultants, and other key advisors that will be relied on in the future. If any are present, allow ample time for questions and discussion.

8. Discuss the 39 Critical Questions. The purpose here is not to solve each issue in advance, but to focus everyone's thinking on the likely difficult ones.

9. If the board of directors has a business plan under review, consider submitting a draft to the family for discussion. When the plan is finalized by the board, a copy may be mailed to family members.

10. Make plans for future family meetings. Future meeting dates could coincide with usual family reunions, holidays, or with regular meetings of the board of directors.

11.   You may want to schedule specific topics about the relationship of the family to the business. Is business talk *always* permitted at *every* family gathering, or are there some family gatherings where it is inappropriate? How are business and pleasure to be mixed? Is a trade convention all work, or may a spouse and children accompany the family member at company expense? What are proper uses of the company plane or company vehicles? What are legitimate expense-account items? What are the appropriate boundaries of business entertainment? How can social occasions be used to further the business? What social obligations to the business do family members have?

A FAMILY COUNCIL

A family council is a formalized family meeting. The threshold question is how to define "family." Shall the family council include spouses? (Because JJ's marriage is strained, the JacMars may hesitate to include any spouses in their family council. This is a delicate judgment call.) Children above a certain age? (At age eighteen, Frank Jr. should probably be included. Perhaps his younger brother, at sixteen, could be invited as an observer.) Fiancees and significant others? Shall in-laws and children have voting privileges?

Then there are the procedural issues: What are the responsibilities of the family council? What matters are appropriate agenda items, and what issues are out of bounds? For example, what input should the family council give on family employment issues (see chapter 10)? What is the *purpose* of the family council? For most families, the council is tied to the family business or to shared family wealth and is used for several purposes:

- *forum-conduit*. In most families, the family council is forum for discussion and a conduit for information. It has no real power to bind family members or the family business. The forum-conduit family council receives information, discusses matters of importance to the family, and distributes information to the family as a whole.

- *deliberate and recommend.* In some families, the family council has the power not only to deliberate but also to make recommendations or to speak on behalf of the family. For example, the family council may recommend entry rules for family employment, or that a family member be hired or fired, or that a family shareholder's stock be redeemed, or that the company name be changed. The recommendations carry the weight of family *influence* but are not binding. The ultimate binding decision is made by management, the board of directors, or the shareholders. Management or the board may wish, however, to solicit the family's opinions on issues that affect the family relationship.

- *vote and decide.* A few family councils are empowered to make decisions that are legally binding on the family and to take action on behalf of the family shareholders. They mediate disagreements and represent the family to the company and to the public. Since the family controls the company, this means that family-council decisions are also binding on company management and upon the board of directors. Ordinarily, the powers of binding family councils are very carefully regulated. Such a family council would not be given the power to sell the company.

- *insulate the board of directors.* It is very important to insulate the board of directors from family conflict. Outside directors will not last long if faced with a steady diet of family friction. This insulation function can be a most valuable contribution of a family council.

- *some delicate agenda items.* Family councils aren't study groups. They may be called on to grapple with tough family issues like those that follow.

FINANCIAL DISTRESS

Family members *do* get into financial trouble—sometimes because of irresponsibility, a life style a family member can't afford, a financial risk that doesn't pan out. And sometimes financial distress arises from uncontrollable circumstances: A family member is laid off, suffers an expensive illness, or loses support as the result of a divorce. When does the family step in? When is it appropriate to tap the family business to relieve that distress? In the JacMars, Frank is overcommitted financially. All of his JacMar shares are pledged to the bank as security for loans he can't repay. Frank Jr. is in college and the second son will enter next year. Frank conceals their money problems from Frances, so she continues to spend—with abandon. What to do?

- Some family companies simply raise dividends. This may help the distress, but it raises the other shareholders' taxes unnecessarily and deprives the company of retained earnings for other purposes.

- Some companies make loans to distressed shareholders. This may work on occasion, say, to generate funds for the down payment on a new home. As a regular practice, however, company loans to family shareholders prompt claims of favoritism from other shareholders—as well as requests from other shareholders for loans.

- Some companies redeem shares from the distressed shareholder. Of course, this requires that a value be placed on the shares, which is a very sensitive issue. If valuation is not a problem, redemption by the company does reduce retained earnings' availability for other purposes.

- Sometimes a strapped shareholder sells shares to other shareholders. This may or may not produce a valuation issue. Even if valuation is not an issue, redemption of one shareholder by another may produce disproportionate ownership among family members, as well as similar requests from other shareholders. The family member who purchases the shares may be accused of playing favorites, or perhaps of taking advantage of a family shareholder's distressed circumstances.

- Some strapped shareholders borrow the funds from a bank or from other family members, pledging their shares as security. If the loan is not repaid, the bank acquires the shares as payment. Foreclosure against a family member can create sticky interpersonal situations.

- There may be other businesslike solutions, but one of the least businesslike is for other family members to cover the debts themselves. This usually puts the distressed family member in an awkward and embarrassing position. For adults, continuing payment of their debts by other family members can be downright demeaning.

There are family members who take unfair advantage of their family's willingness to help. They continue life styles they can't afford, expecting the family always to clean up their financial debris. This is a bad situation for all and calls for tough love.

Frank doesn't understand why the company can't increase his salary (now equal to his brother's) to tide him over the expensive college years. Jack bitterly criticizes Frank's financial plight, and Margaret defends Frank. It's hard to administer tough love in a financial setting to an adult child who is raising your grandchildren, whose marriage would be stretched by imposing financial restraints. But who will take that responsibility when the family member won't take it?

This is not a matter for JacMar's board of directors. Frank's plight is a mixed family-and-business issue for the family council, which can administer tough love in an evenhanded manner that neither Jack nor Margaret could muster. JJ and Karen, in consultation with Frank and Frances can probably work it out, as adults.

DIVORCE

It may be the founder's divorce or the divorce of the heir-apparent. The divorced couple may work in the business. In almost every setting, divorce profoundly disrupts a business family but it has become so common that business families have come to expect it and even to insist on prenuptial agreements. A prenuptial agreement is a contract between two people engaged to be married that regulates their marital property. A common provision in prenuptial agreements keeps the family shares from passing to the other spouse if there is a divorce. Couples who have been married before understand the need for prenuptial agreements, especially if both have children from prior marriages. But couples engaged for the first time can have great emotional difficulty with prenuptial agreements. They are turned off by a legal document that contemplates their divorce. How hard to press engaged couples to enter prenuptial agreements is an important issue for family councils.

JJ and Judy have no prenuptial agreement. Although a court might award Judy the ownership of JacMar stock as part of a property settlement, a buy-sell agreement could require Judy to offer those shares to other members of the family at a predetermined price formula. Judy might have been willing to sign such an agreement before her marriage began to sour, but not now. Marital difficulties can wreak havoc on a business family *even if the spouses never divorce*. Marital strife that threatens the family business is a proper subject for a family council.

Irresponsible Conduct

Now and then, a family member does something that is terribly irresponsible. Some steal from the business, others become involved in crimes or scandals, some tell family secrets or business secrets, or do other intentional harm. Their irresponsibility is often connected with substance abuse, gambling, or shady financial deals. Whatever the conduct, there are repercussions in the family. Perhaps the matter can be kept from the public, but certain people in the family should be informed. If irresponsible conduct becomes public knowledge, the family may need to take a public position. If the family transgressor owes restitution, should the family help, and how? Most of all, how will the family *support* its errant member? Like it or not he or she will still be a family member and ostracism is old-fashioned. What's the best plan for continuing nurture? Irresponsible conduct is a prime issue for a family council.

Striking Out on Their Own

Now and then, a family member just doesn't fit in the family business. Whatever the reason, some family members feel driven to make it on their own. They may not intend disloyalty to the family, but they must be loyal to themselves. What to do? Recall Jack's dilemma. He was fired from his first job because he couldn't stand being supervised by "incompetents." Given Jack's personality, it's unlikely he would have been content working for *anyone*. Jack needed to work for himself.

Setting up family members in their own ventures can take a variety of forms. For some, it's enough to have autonomy over part of the family business—a geographical region, a product line, a new venture. Others can buy a portion of the family business, own it themselves, run it themselves. Such was the case with David Ingram, one of three brothers who was heir to Ingram Industries that, until restructuring in June 1996, was among the top ten private U.S. companies. The two older brothers, Orrin and John, sold Ingram Entertainment to their younger brother.

Sometimes the company can acquire an existing business to be managed by a family member. In other instances, the family may provide financing and other support. Questions of favoritism arise when a family member leaves the fold. Is the family allocating too many resources to satisfy the whims of one of its members? What is fair to those who remain in the family business or to those who don't work there but who own stock? Whatever the venture, it should make business sense, with reasonable potential for profit and success. Parking family members in business playpens isn't fair to them or others. The venture's impact on total family wealth should be considered. If the venture fails, will failure further drain family financial resources? If it succeeds, will profits accrue to other family members who have backed the enterprise? Is the venture taking a disproportionate share of family resources, family attention, family concern? How will they handle the emotional reactions of other family members? Somehow the parable of the Prodigal Son comes to mind. Who grapples with these questions? The family council.

Inside Your Business Family . . .
How does your family resolve disputes? Does your family negotiate? Does your family fight? Does your family just pretend that disputes don't exist?

Does your family company hold annual shareholders' meetings? Would your next annual shareholders' meeting be a good opportunity to hold a family business retreat?

Write down three sites that might be appropriate for a family retreat.

Would your family need an outside facilitator?

What information about your company, other than financial, would interest most members of your family? How could that information be presented? Who should present it?

What tasks should your family undertake with regard to the family business? Exploration of an outside board? Entry rules? Sale of the business? Compensation of family members? Dividends? A family council?

How might your family organize its family council? Who would be the first members? What aspect of family or business life would each represent? When and where would they meet? Which function would be best for your family council? Forum-conduit? Deliberate and recommend? Vote and decide? How might your family insulate your outside directors from family disputes?

Is your business family currently helping some family member in financial distress? If so, how is the money being made available? By loan? Increased dividends? Redemption of shares? Guarantee of bank loans? Excessive compensation? Should your family have a policy about financial assistance from the company? If so, what kind of financial assistance policy would work best for your family?

Have there been divorces in your family? If so, how have these divorces affected your business family? Are there shaky marriages in your family? If so, how do they affect your business family? Could stock in the business become involved in a marital property settlement? How does the possibility of divorce affect your family? For example, do family members avoid talking business with in-laws? If so, how does this affect in-laws' loyalty to the business? To the family?

Suppose a member of your family were to do something extremely irresponsible? How would that be handled in your family? How would the family handle the publicity? Who would speak for the family? Would the family be more likely to support its errant member or to ostracize? How might that irresponsible conduct affect the family business?

Suppose a family member wants to open his or her own business and asks for financial backing from the family. How would your family handle this request? Would your family be likely to encourage or discourage members to strike out on their own? Who would make the decision about financial backing? Would that decision be discussed with other family members? Would that decision be supported by other family members?

20

KEY EMPLOYEES

Our assets go home at night. Without them, we're nothing.
—*Keith Crain, Vice Chairman, Crain Communications, Inc.*[21]

Critical Question 32: *How do we protect the contributions of unrelated key employees?*

Critical Question 33: *To what extent do we involve key employees in family disagreements?*

Critical Question 34: *What obligations do we have to prized employees?*

Critical Question 35: *Should key employees own stock in our family business?*

Critical Question 36: *Might one key employee be the next leader of the business?*

Critical Question 37: *How do we treat loyal employees whose productivity or value to the company has declined?*

Successful entrepreneurs are loners? Not so.

Every successful entrepreneur owes his or her success to key employees. Jack's key employees have bet their families on the success of JacMar Corporation. So far they are winning.

ASK AL

Al and Jack have been personal friends since Al joined JacMar eleven years ago. Both are engineers, both define themselves by their work. They begin with coffee together every morning and have lunch together almost every day in the JacMar cafeteria. Sometimes Jack unburdens on Al, who listens sympathetically but rarely offers advice.

Al is a good people-person who employees like. He is a good second in command, he carries lots of messages to and from Jack. Dedicated to the unwritten company motto of "Please Jack," Al seldom disagrees openly with Jack and sees his mission as "Jack's will be done."

Al is almost like a member of Jack's family; he and Jack have vacationed together with their wives. Margaret trusts Al implicitly. Perhaps like her sons, Al is underworked and overpaid and lacks the drive that would earn him a similar position outside JacMar Corporation. But Al has invested his working lifetime in the company. Al and his family depend on JacMar Corporation as much as the company depends upon him. He has a mortgage, tuition payments for college-age children, a company retirement plan—all dependent upon the continued success of JacMar Corporation. Never underestimate Jack's loyalty to Al, who has stuck with Jack during some very hard times. Al is a very good soldier.

Al is wise and secure in his position. Unlike some other key employees, he doesn't try to magnify his importance by too-close supervision of subordinates, and he knows how much space to give the people who report to him. Al knows how to delegate, and he does. He isn't out to build an empire or to wrest the company away from Jack. Al knows how to handle bad news, how to present it to Jack, how to withstand Jack's temper tantrums. Al is a *very* good soldier.

Al ran the company for four months during Jack's heart surgery a few years ago. Day-to-day, Al performed very well. He steered the course and changed nothing. He consulted regularly with Jack and helped ease much of Jack's anxiety. JJ was greatly disappointed that Al was chosen to run the company during his father's illness, but Al was Margaret's choice, also. No one thought that JJ was ready.

ASK NELSON

Jack has another idea: He has been talking to Nelson. In secret. Jack is very impressed by Nelson, who is an engineer with an MBA from a top business school. Nelson's career has been with public companies, and he was in line for president of his company until it was unexpectedly acquired by foreign investors, when he lost the race to the top. Jack is convinced that Nelson could succeed him and would do an excellent job of leading the company's growth. Nelson would keep up the quality of their products and take care of the employees who are Jack's friends— they could trust Nelson with their careers. Al could keep the company going, "steer the course," but Al lacks vision, decisiveness, a willingness to *risk*. Jack doesn't accept Al's suggestion that JJ could run the company. In Jack's view, *his son is too much like Al*. JJ is too much a manager, too little a visionary; too much a consensus builder, too little a leader; too much a sender of weak signals, too little a deliverer of strong messages.

Jack and Nelson aren't exactly negotiating, but they are close to it. Jack has been surprised by Nelson's aggressive approach. He would demand a large salary, a tough employment contract, an expansive benefits package, and extensive options to acquire stock in JacMar Corporation. Nelson suspects a low survival rate of nonfamily CEOs in family businesses, but he is confident he can run JacMar Corporation successfully. He is not so confident he can get along with the family, especially if other family members want his job.

What Jack cannot foresee are the consequences of Nelson's classic public-company management style. Nelson is very close to the numbers, results oriented. He is a goal setter, planner, delegator who would cut the fat out of JacMar Corporation, lay off unneeded employees, work the rest of them harder and smarter, do away with company cars, close the company cafeteria. Few JacMar employees would encounter him on a daily basis, and they would perceive Nelson as aloof, cold, impersonal. The company would prosper, of course. Their pay and benefits would increase. But it wouldn't be the same. They couldn't go directly to the boss, he wouldn't come directly to them. The familial atmosphere of JacMar Corporation would forever change.

WHAT IF ...

Jack is pondering. Suppose Jack hires Nelson as CEO then withdraws gradually from daily responsibilities over two to three years. Suppose Al remains as general manager. Would Nelson replace Al, or find a way to work with him? Would JJ work for Nelson? Would Nelson tolerate Frank's office on the golf course? Would Nelson summarily discharge the alcoholic salesman instead of, as Frank has suggested, granting him early retirement?

Suppose JacMar grants substantial stock options to Nelson based on company performance under his leadership. Would this unduly upset the family? Are Nelson's demands for stock ownership reasonable, or should he be satisfied with a "phantom stock" arrangement?

How would the family accept Nelson's changes? Who would handle family complaints about Nelson? Would it always be Jack? How would Margaret react to Nelson? After Jack's death, would she use her voting power to replace him with JJ? Or with Karen? Who would monitor Nelson's performance? Who would hold him accountable, and how would they do it?

BUSINESS VALUES VS. FAMILY VALUES

Hiring a nonfamily CEO focuses the tensions between business values and family values. Nelson personifies business values, and he would run JacMar Corporation as a business. But Nelson must adapt to a new business culture and learn to run JacMar

Corporation as a *family-owned* business. He must learn to respond to a new set of nuances and become personally sensitive to family whims and prejudices. Nelson must learn when to resist family pressures and when to capitulate, and modify his nothing-but-business instincts in order to lead a successful family-owned business.

The family must accommodate Nelson, if he is to succeed. As a fellow shareholder, Nelson will try to serve the family by improving the bottom line, but that means he won't woo them with entitlements and will cut back on perks. He will rule more from the head than from the heart, his loyalties tied more to finances than to personalities—he will be loyal *in his way*. The family will learn how to recognize, even appreciate, his loyalties. But it won't be the same. Both the outside board and the family council will be challenged.

A number of pieces must fall into place before Nelson succeeds. Jack must discuss with Margaret his interest in Nelson. He must determine whether Margaret can let go of her dream that one of her sons will succeed Jack. If Margaret consents, Jack will need the support of his children and, ultimately, the blessing of his outside board of directors, who will make the final decision about Nelson.

Inside Your Business Family . . .

If your business leader were completely disabled for six months, who would run the company? Is there an emergency plan that names a temporary successor? Is the plan in writing? Has it been published to the family? If your business leader were to die, could that temporary successor keep the business operating successfully?

Could a nonrelative function well as CEO of your company? Would your family accept him or her? What changes would the CEO want to make? What changes would your family resist?

21

THE COMMUNITY

We're a face, not just a company with somebody who's a manager and who represents somebody who represents somebody who represents some stockholders down the road.
—*Kathryn Klinger, President, Georgette Klinger Salons, Inc.*[22]

Critical Question 38: *What are our responsibilities to the community?*

Critical Question 39: *How do we cope with our public image and the public's expectations of us?*

The list of larger contributors to the United Way in your community is heavy with family businesses. Family businesses emphasize concern for others, and most are very good corporate citizens. Family businesses furnish leadership to charitable, civic, religious organizations.

THE COMMUNITY FAMILY

The "family touch" extends not only to employees but also to the community at large. As a memorial to his mother, one family business leader opened a day-care center to serve his own employees and employees of neighboring businesses. Another family endowed a chair at a major university in honor of their business leader during his lifetime. Honoring the community and the business family expresses good stewardship of the American Dream.

In recessions, public companies cut back their support to community activities, but most family businesses hang in there because they are local. Their investment in the community pays dividends they can see. JJ is very active in civic affairs, in part as a way to find a leadership role that has been denied him (so far) at JacMar Corporation. But in community service, JJ has also found something he didn't expect—his *self-esteem*.

JJ's civic activities have earned him a wide circle of friends and acquaintances. Thrust into leadership roles JJ has become more outgoing, with a heightened sense of responsibility to others. If JJ succeeds his father in the business, he will have to cut back on time devoted to civic leadership. He will miss it. Community service has been a valuable mentor.

PUBLIC IMAGE

Business families live in a fish bowl, particularly if they are large employers in the community—some still operate company towns. Public image is important to business families, and wise families *cultivate* their public image. But public images are fragile; bad news about the company can quickly erode one. An industrial accident, a lawsuit, an environmental problem can do damage. Knowing this, wise companies work positively on their public image and build up a reservoir of good will. They don't just do damage control, they cultivate the media with favorable news stories and spend time and money telling the good things about their company.

A positive public image reflects directly on family members. If the name on the water tower triggers favorable responses in the community, family members sense it in their own lives. Members of a business family need public respect, but it must be earned, cultivated, nurtured. It may be hard to tell whether family members "wear" the business or *are* the business. The best family businesses reflect sound family values to the public by careful and constructive attention to the public image.

Inside Your Business Family . . .

To what extent does your family business serve your community? List the charities to which your company contributes. List the civic and charitable organizations in which family members serve in a personal capacity.

In what ways has community service enhanced the value of family employees to your business? In what ways could community service be valuable to your company?

Does your company encourage employees to take their part in the community? If so, in what ways? Are they recognized for their service? Are they identified to the public as company employees? Does the company match their contributions to worthy causes?

Does your business have a public relations policy? A public relations advisor? Does your business actively seek favorable media attention, or are you limited to "damage control" when things go wrong and the public finds out?

What is your business family doing to store up a reservoir of public good will?

22

JACK'S DREAM

I worry about keeping our culture, keeping the things we believe in.

—*Sam Walton, Founder, Wal-Mart Inc.*[23]

Jack doesn't know the origin of his dream, but it visits him often. Every night at bedtime he wonders if it will reappear.

The scene is a one-ring circus. In the center of the ring is Jack, dressed as a strong man in animal skins and black boots laced nearly to his knees. A circus performance is in progress.

Jack, the strong man, holds a huge plank over his head. Kneeling on the plank in rough pyramid fashion are Margaret, their children and grandchildren, and JacMar's key employees and their families. Jack's muscles are beginning to fatigue. He is bathed in sweat. Veins pop out on his forehead. His chest hurts. His strength is giving way. The plank and its passengers begin to sink. Jack steals a look at the audience. Some are crying. Some are laughing. Some are just staring at poor Jack. . . .

Jack wakes with a start.

Jack's dream is not exactly a nightmare. But it isn't pleasant either. Jack told a psychologist about his dream and asked what the dream meant.

"I don't know," said the psychologist, "but let's work on it. Close your eyes and try to recreate your dream in your imagination. This time, push on to its conclusion." Jack closed his eyes and recreated the dream as best he could.

This time, as his muscles were giving way under the heavy plank and its passengers, his load suddenly began to lighten. Al hopped down and helped Jack hold the plank. Next Frank, then JJ followed. The plank grew lighter. Soon others joined them.

Jack could drop his hands now. Others were holding his burden.

Someone helped Margaret down. She took Jack's arm and they walked triumphantly together around the circus ring—to thundering applause. They were savoring and celebrating the American Dream.

Inside Your Business Family . . .

How does Jack's dream strike you? Have you dreamed about your family business? If so, do you remember a particular dream? Does it recur? Have you told anyone about it? Have you tried to find meaning in your dream?

Turn back to JJ's dream in chapter 16. Which dream is a nightmare—Jack's dream or his son's dream?

23

FROM QUESTIONS TO ANSWERS

My family is a classic example of a founder who is so swept up by
his career of being a titan of American industry that he didn't take
time to raise his children or teach them the family business.
    —*Patrick Reynolds (Heir to RJR Nabisco, Inc.),*
    Founding President, Citizens for a Smokefree America[24]

The JacMar Agenda didn't come together during their first
retreat, so the family has been working on it for several months.
At best, it is only an interim agenda. There is still much family
work to do.

The process hasn't been smooth or seamless: discussions still
wander off the point, some talk too much, there is a lot of repeti-
tion. One, then another, declares the whole exercise hopeless, a
waste of time. But bit by ragged bit, they have stayed with it.
Over time, their meeting skills have improved. They have
become much better listeners. They take turns preparing the
meeting agenda, take turns leading the discussion. When things
become unbearably tense, they have learned to "go around the
table"—asking each person to comment before proceeding.

Their family work is well begun, but far from finished. The
JacMars have become more conscious of each others' feelings

and moods. They understand that Jack's view of reality isn't necessarily their own and are working toward a family relationship that honors their different views of reality. It seems that they hadn't *really* talked together as adults before, instead behaving like grownups and adolescent children. Now everyone has grown some. In the process the JacMars have surprised themselves. In a recent meeting, Jack and JJ reached an impasse. Everyone waited for Jack's customary put down. Instead, Jack said to JJ, "Maybe we're going to differ about that." That's progress!

The family has used the 39 Critical Questions to outline their family work. The JacMar Agenda contains their interim answers. They are still meeting, still working.

THE JACMAR AGENDA

1. *Are we committed to the future of our family business?*

We ask each family member to describe in writing the role he or she desires to play in the future of JacMar Corporation. Everyone is encouraged to be candid and forthright and to discuss both personal and business needs as they relate to the company. We will disclose any limitations on the roles we wish to play. If we want no part, we are free to say so. Our commitment to JacMar Corporation is wholly separate from our loyalty to the family.

2. *Are we obligated to work there indefinitely, or may we pursue other careers?*

We will prepare written entry rules for employment that will apply to present and future family employees. Those entry rules will make it clear whether younger generation members are required, encouraged, permitted, discouraged, or forbidden to work in the company. It is likely that our entry rules will encourage every family member to pursue the career that best fits interest and aptitude, whether in the company or elsewhere.

3. *Do we want to own the business, or should it be sold?*

Jack and Margaret encourage their children to continue family ownership of JacMar Corporation. However, we will obtain a professional appraisal of the value of the company for sale purposes and determine whether our company is really salable. We will "walk through" a hypothetical sale of the business and attempt to visualize the impact of sale on the family.

4. *How do we decide which family members will be employed by the company?*

We will ascertain which family members want a career in the JacMar Corporation. We will be realistic about their career opportunities, both inside and outside the company. We will adopt written entry rules for family members who wish to work in the business, circulate the rules to each family member, and revise them as our circumstances change. Our entry rules will recognize our devotion to the work ethic and that sweat equity must be earned. Subject to the entry rules, every family member will be eligible for employment. Continuation of employment is not guaranteed but is earned by daily job performance. Any family member is free to terminate his or her employment at JacMar Corporation at any time without disclosing a reason.

5. *Must we offer every family member a job?*

No family member is entitled to employment at JacMar Corporation. We will decide in advance how to handle requests for exceptions to our entry rules. There may be compelling reasons to make an occasional exception. The family council will consider requests for exceptions before the employment decision is made.

6. *Should in-laws or other relatives be invited to work in the business?*

Our entry rules will state whether, for career purposes, in-laws can expect to be treated the same as blood relatives. If in-law employees are to be treated differently from other employees, these differences will be spelled out in the entry rules.

7. *What education or work preparation should be required of family members who work in the business?*

Our entry rules will contain sensible educational requirements for family members who desire careers with the company. We recognize that different persons have different educational aptitudes and different educational motivations. Some burn out, some are late bloomers. In most cases, family members should undertake significant outside work experience before they are hired by the company. Our entry rules will set out minimum requirements for outside work and procedures for making exceptions in worthy cases.

8. How do we assign titles and work responsibility?

We agree to assign family work titles that accurately describe our actual job responsibilities. Each family employee will have a realistic, written job description. We will offer and require each family employee and family applicant to undergo expert career testing and evaluation, career assessment, and career counseling. Work responsibilities will be assigned by management consistent with the needs of the business.

9. How should we evaluate and pay family members who work in the business?

We will try to offer each family employee an opportunity for coaching and guidance from a senior nonfamily key employee. Where appropriate, the senior employee will review the family member's performance. We will install performance review systems for all employees, and make no exceptions for family members. We will demand candor from those who review the performance of family members and insulate the reviewers from family pressures. We will adhere to a consistent compensation policy for family members, tying compensation to actual work responsibility (sweat equity) rather than financial need or maintenance of life style. Family relationship (blood equity) may be considered in determining bonuses. Family employees will be given an opportunity for input before family bonus decisions are made.

10. What should we do if a family member doesn't perform or leaves the business?

We will adopt a strict policy requiring family employees to report on time, to perform their duties satisfactorily, and to become contributing members of the company. We will not be lenient with family members who don't measure up. Family members are free to terminate their employment with the company at will. If a family employee must be involuntarily terminated, it will be handled diplomatically and quietly. A family member wishing to question his or her termination may appeal to the family council.

11. *How do we select the next leader of the business?*

Selection of corporate officers is the primary duty of our board of directors. Our family council may recommend qualified family members for any corporate office to our board of directors, including candidates for CEO. A board decision on the selection of corporate officers may be overruled by the family council, but only with concurrence of shareholders owning at least 60 percent of the voting stock of the company. Qualified members of the family eligible for any corporate office include both males and females, regardless of birth order.

12. *When do we decide who will be the next leader of the company?*

Selection of a successor CEO shall be made as early as feasible to allow the maximum opportunity for training and transition. Employees will be advised of the selection early on. The timing of public announcement will be determined by the board, after consultation with the family council.

13. *When and how should leadership transition take place?*

Leadership transition will take place in accordance with a transition plan to be adopted by the Board, after consultation with the family council. The transition plan will include a timetable for transition, phased-in training, team building for incumbent and future leaders, and a detailed arrangement for drawing upon their experience and expertise.

14. *How do we evaluate our new leader's job performance?*

Review of management performance is a primary duty of our board of directors. The family council will not participate in management review, except in unusual circumstances.

15. *How do we provide meaningful careers for other family members who are not chosen to lead?*

Our entry rules will encourage all qualified family members to seek careers in the company, subject to the entry rules. Each qualified family member is entitled to opportunities for meaningful work. Work assignments will be made by company officers elected by the board of directors. A family member who is dissatisfied with his or her work assignment shall appeal first to his or her superior. If still dissatisfied, a family member may appeal to the family council.

16. *Who should serve on our board of directors? Family members? Employees? Our outside advisors? Others?*

Our directors serve at the pleasure of the shareholders. Our by-laws call for seven directors, one of whom will always be the CEO. Four directors will be family shareholders recommended by the family council. There will always be two outside directors, who will be selected for their expertise and value to the company. An outside director may not be a family member, an employee of the company, an outside advisor to the family or the company, a customer or supplier to the company, or have any conflict of interest with the company or the family.

17. *How should our board of directors function?*

We desire an active board of directors. We will keep our directors informed, actively seek their counsel, and carefully weigh their advice. We will not ask our directors to intervene in family disagreements. An outside director will always chair our Compensation Committee and the Audit Committee.

18. *What should we expect of our directors?*

We expect all of our directors to attend and participate in all board meetings and committee meetings. We expect them to be candid and forceful in rendering their opinions and advice.

19. *Who should own stock in the business?*

We have decided to limit shareholders to blood descendants of the founder, wherever possible. To that end, we have requested our attorneys to draft a suitable buy-sell agreement that requires any shareholder to first offer his or her shares to other family members before transferring the shares to outsiders.

20. *Should all children own equally, whether or not they work in the business?*

We realize that there may be circumstances in which equal ownership of company stock may not be desirable. Ideally, stock ownership should be limited to family members who are active in the business. For estate-planning purposes, we agree that future stock ownership should be frankly discussed between those who give and those who receive.

21. *What dividends or perquisites (perks) should shareholders receive?*

We understand the difference between blood equity and sweat equity. Compensation is in return for sweat equity. We advocate generous but reasonable compensation to family members who work in the business. We agree that family employees are entitled to perks commensurate with those provided to unrelated employees in comparable well-managed companies. We realize that, to the extent family employees are overcompensated or receive excessive perks, they reduce the value of other family members' shares. We advocate reasonable perks for family members who do not work in the business, especially to take advantage of company groups or discounts. However, perks are not substitutes for reasonable dividends. Declaration of dividends is the primary responsibility of the board of directors. So long as we are an S Corporation for tax purposes, shareholders should receive dividends sufficient to cover their personal tax liability on company earnings. Further dividends are a function of blood equity. We recognize that payment of dividends reduces retained earnings otherwise available for financing company growth. We further recognize, however, that by retaining their shares, family shareholders are investing their inheritance in our company and should receive a reasonable return. When earnings are sufficient, we expect our board to declare reasonable dividends in excess of shareholder tax liability, consistent with the company's immediate needs for capital.

22. *How do we balance the interests of inside family shareholders (who work in the business) with the interests of outside family shareholders (who don't work in the business)?*

We will take steps to minimize tensions between inside and outside shareholders. We acknowledge the blood equity in shareholders beyond the first generation and in all dividends. We will establish a free flow of information about the company. Financial information will be circulated regularly to all shareholders. Full disclosure will be encouraged, including the salaries, benefits, and perks paid to all family employees. Consistent with security and confidentiality, outside shareholders will be reasonably informed of current developments inside the company. The views and recommendations of outside shareholders will be courteously and seriously received. Outside shareholders recognize that there is ordinarily no market for their minority shares; that an interested buyer would likely offer a deeply discounted price because of their minority position.

23. *What do we do if a family member wants to sell out?*

No family member is obligated to continue holding company shares. Any family member may donate shares to descendants, or may sell shares after first offering them pro rata to other family shareholders. Our pending buy-sell agreement will specify a fair pricing formula should other family members elect to purchase. Outside shareholders understand that the maximum price they could expect for their shares would result only from the sale of the entire company.

24. *How should we deal with family disagreements? (Between individuals? Between members of the same or different generations?)*

Though we are all adults, we have not always acted toward each other like adults, nor have we always treated each other as adults. At times, older generation members have treated younger generation members like children. At times, younger generation members have behaved childishly. We resolve to change that behavior. We will form a family council to deal with mixed family and business matters and other important issues involving the family as a whole.

25. *How do we teach in-laws and younger generation family members about the values and traditions of our business and our family?*

We will expand our annual shareholders' meeting into a regular family retreat. We will spend some retreat time on:

- family history and the history of our company

- reviewing company operations and plans

- relaxing and enjoying each other

- celebrating the good fortune our family business has brought to all of us

We will involve in-laws and older children in these sessions.

26. *Who will lead family activities in the next generation?*

We acknowledge the vital roles of the "emotional officers," male or female, in our family. They bind us together. They convene us and nurture us as a family. They, too, need successors. We will involve younger generation members and their spouses in planning our annual retreats and in hosting other family occasions.

27. *How do we help family members in financial distress?*

The personal financial needs of a family member are a legitimate family concern. While our family values dictate prudence in financial matters, our family will respond to the legitimate financial needs of its members. Financial needs addressed through the company must be first approved by the family council. Loans of company funds may be made if they bear interest at prevailing interest rates and are secured by the borrower's company stock. The company may purchase (redeem) all or part of a family member's shares to generate funds for appropriate reasons. Family assistance to one member in distress does not, of itself, entitle any other family member to similar assistance.

28. *What other responsibilities do we have to other family members?*

Though adult and financially independent, we bear a continuing responsibility for each other's welfare and happiness. We could not obtain such support, encouragement, trust, loyalty, and love outside our family. We did not choose each other, nor do we always approve of each other's behavior. Yet we are bound together for mutual respect and support, forever. We will do our best to resolve our differences without prejudicing our children.

29. *What do we do if there is a divorce in the family?*

We recognize the existence of marital estrangement and divorce. Where possible, we will be parties to reconciliation. We will do our best to minimize divorce's adverse effects on the couple, and particularly upon their children. To maintain stock ownership solely among the descendants of our founder, we encourage premarital and postmarital property agreements and property settlements to that effect.

30. *What if a family member breaks the law or is seriously irresponsible?*

Unlawful or unduly irresponsible conduct will be considered by the family council. The family council offers its advice to family members and has the legal power to commit a family member for treatment or observation against his or her will. If the irresponsible conduct attracts public attention, the family council will preapprove all media statements made on behalf of the family. We will consider a Family Code of Conduct that spells out minimum standards of behavior for family members with regard to the company. Central to the code of conduct will be our agreement to abide by the decisions of the board of directors and the officers our board elects.

31. *How do we support family members in their own business ventures?*

We encourage new business ventures by individual family members. We recognize that family wealth may be required to launch such ventures and that investment of company resources in such ventures may be appropriate. Family members desiring company resources to launch a new venture must first present a detailed proposal to the family council, which will forward its recommendation to the board of directors, which shall have final authority to act on the request.

32. *How do we protect the contributions of unrelated key employees?*

Our business success is due in large part to valued employees who are not family members. They have chosen to work for our company instead of others. They have been generously compensated for their contributions, and we acknowledge our tendency to overcompensate them. We defer to our board of directors to determine their compensation, under the guidance of the Compensation Committee.

33. *To what extent do we involve key employees in family disagreements?*

Although key employees may witness family disagreements, we will not embarrass them by involving them in intrafamily conflicts. We will not seek to enlist them on behalf of one family member against another, nor penalize them for not taking sides.

34. *What obligations do we have to prized employees?*

We express important family values in the treatment of prized employees. By investing their careers in our company, they have placed their own families at the risk of our success. We appreciate their confidence and the sacrifices they have made in our behalf. We realize that many of their contributions cannot be compensated in money.

35. *Should key employees own stock in our family business?*

We do not favor allowing unrelated employees to acquire stock in the company, but favor contracts with key employees that would give them some financial benefits equivalent to stock ownership.

36. *Might one key employee be the next leader of our business?*

Although qualified family candidates are favored, we acknowledge that a nonfamily member could be the best choice for CEO. Subject to veto by the family council, selection of the next leader of the business is within the discretion of the board of directors.

37. *How do we treat loyal employees whose productivity or value to the company has declined?*

We recognize that unproductive employees, including unproductive family employees, can create adverse situations. The company has no obligation to keep an employee who is not fulfilling his or her job description.

38. *What are our responsibilities to the community?*

Our company has always acknowledged its community obligations. We support worthy causes with money and with the time and talents of our employees. We should continue to seek out opportunities to serve and support the community and to identify the company and the family with such support.

39. *How do we cope with our public image and the public's expectations of us?*

We recognize that the general public associates each of us with our company, whether or not we are company employees. Likewise, the personal conduct of each family member reflects on the company. Our public image is precious; it is our public heritage. Our reputation with the business community is irreplaceable. We will make all reasonable efforts to preserve our favorable public image. Our Code of Conduct will reflect that concern.

JACMAR CORPORATION
CODE OF CONDUCT FOR THE FAMILY

The company is a family enterprise. It must be successful as a business but operated consistent with our core family values.

This requires balancing the interests of the business and those of the family.

The business is a cooperative effort. While we each are entitled to our respective individuality and views and the right to express them freely, each of us agrees to abide by the final decisions of those in authority.

We wish to continue all stock ownership in the family. We agree that only the founders and their descendants should own stock; that stock ownership is not appropriate for in-laws or unrelated persons.

We have agreed to elect a board of directors, at least two of whom are not members of the family. The principal function of our board is to make company policy and to review management. We agree to be bound by their decisions in those matters. It would not be appropriate to involve unrelated board members in family disputes, and we agree not to call upon the board to settle them. Our board of directors is charged with selecting leaders for the company. We agree to abide by their decisions and to accept the authority of the persons they choose.

We agree that whoever is managing the business is entitled to control it. We also agree that each of us is entitled to invest his or her personal fortune as he or she chooses. To that end we have executed or agree to execute an agreement permitting active family members to buy the shares of inactive members at a fair price.

We cannot take everything we want from the business. The business should provide each family member active in it with a decent standard of living. We recognize that those who contribute more to the business are entitled to more compensation. As officers of the business, we agree to accept our compensation as determined by the board of directors. As shareholders of the business, we agree to accept those dividends and distributions declared by the board of directors. We agree to take no more out of the business than is authorized by our board of directors.

We understand that each of us has different interests, skills, and talents that fit us for particular contributions to the business. We want to contribute our best selves to the business. We agree to maximize our gifts for the benefit of the business by training, employment assignment, and otherwise.

Entrepreneurship is at the very heart of our business. We agree to encourage and offer advice to family members who choose to pursue independent business interests. However, so long as a family member is active in the family business, he shall devote his full working time and attention to it.

JACMAR CORPORATION
FAMILY MISSION STATEMENT

We want our business to grow and prosper.

We want ownership of our business to continue in succeeding generations of the family.

We want qualified family members to be active in the management of the business. We are committed to providing career opportunities for the founders' descendants and their families.

We want all family members to gain a real appreciation of the risks and rewards of being in business.

We want our business to continue with the high standards of quality, service, and responsibility instilled in all of us by its founders.

We want to experience the sacrifices and rewards that family members can enjoy by working closely together toward common goals.

We want to maximize the quality of life to be enjoyed by our families and succeeding generations.

We intend to encourage all family members to develop and apply their particular skills and aptitudes to the business and to compensate each fairly for his or her contribution. As long as they are active in the business full-time, all descendants of the founders should be provided with opportunities for ownership in the business.

We intend to extend to unrelated employees a sense of belonging to our "extended family" by sharing with them our appreciation and financial rewards and benefits that will continue a mutually prosperous and enriching long-term relationship.

The JacMars will take a step backwards now and then. Occasionally they will fall back into their old ways. They will become discouraged from time to time, but having come this far, their prospects are quite good.

24

TO MY SUCCESSOR . . .

There was an episode on "Dallas" . . . Bobby saying to Jock, "But, Daddy, you gave me the power to run Ewing Oil." Jock looked at him and said, "Bobby, nobody can give you power."
—*Eric Johnson, CEO, Johnson Products Company*[25]

Just before Jack called the board meeting to order, one of JacMar's new outside directors handed him a copy of the following letter from an unknown father to an unknown son.* Jack keeps the letter in the lap drawer of his desk. He reads it from time to time.

Dear Son:

This letter is to outline some of the issues and sensitivities that pertain to your joining us.

First of all, we are interested in you because our key management believes that you possess the personal skills, background, and education to be an effective member of our team, and that you can become a significant contributor to our future growth

---

*This is an authentic copy of real letter from father to son, entrusted to the author for publication.

and success. The fact that you are my son is secondary. However, this can create both pleasure and problems for both of us. While I cannot anticipate all the possibilities, the following are some guidelines that I propose we follow if you accept employment here.

1.   As an employee/son you can expect some quiet resentment from certain employees until you establish yourself as an independent contributor to the company. Ignore this and concentrate on learning our business, working hard, attempting to contribute, and just being yourself, not my son.

2.   My management style is to work closely with those who report to me and to be interested in helping all other employees. I expect to be helpful to you in training and work-related problem solving. But it will be as with other employees who do not report to me, at arm's length.

3.   As my son, you may be subjected to others trying to use you as a messenger to get their ideas to the boss, or get information from me. Don't allow yourself to be a part of those types of conversations. I want your value to the company to be through your achievement, not your family ties.

4.   To help our relationship, I suggest that we do not discuss those business issues at home that we would not discuss at the office, including office gossip. In other words, if you are working with a new customer and want to discuss that during our social time together, that is fine. However, it is not good for you to be privy to information that you would not normally need or use in doing your job. This issue applies even more to your wife. I suggest that she should not approach me to negotiate on your behalf, but rather help you identify and discuss such issues with your direct supervisor. It would be very "healthy" if, on business issues, she considered me as the president of the company for which you work and be as selective in such discussions as she would be with the president of any other company for whom you might work. In return I will try to be sensitive to her interest and concerns. This is a key issue that pertains to family harmony and to your self-

esteem in achieving success through your personal efforts and excellence rather than from family ties and connections.

5.   In joining the company, there are no strings attached. This is an opportunity for you, and we cannot predict where it will lead. However, we should agree on the following:

a) You are free to leave if ever or whenever you find a better opportunity. It will not affect my bond or feelings for you as a father. I want the best for you at all times.

b) If we find that this is not the right company or environment (small versus large. entrepreneurial versus corporate) for you, we will help you find a better fit. As my son I expect that this would not affect your bond or feeling for me.

c) From the outset I have run this company for the best long-term benefit of all the investors. I plan to continue this even after most of the current outside investors are gone. This means that I may choose to take the company public or to sell the company. While I do not have such plans at this time, I may in the future. I ask that you accept my right to do so and to understand that inheriting part of my estate is your birthright, but inheriting the company is not.

d) In joining the company, I expect you to work hard, apply yourself, have commitment, and use all of your skills and education toward attaining the company's goals. As long as you do that, you will have met my expectations of you as my son. I am proud of you now, and I shall be so in the future. I do not have any other expectations, and you should not place the weight of any other expectations that you think I have upon yourself. For example, to satisfy me you do not have to become a great entrepreneur or the next president of the company. If it happens, it will happen. My affection and respect for you are not based on such goals.

e) We cannot predict the future status of you, your sister, and your respective families. It is therefore not sound for me to establish ground rules pertaining to relationships and financial arrangements. However, please be aware that at some point in the future I may establish such rules. Their objective will be to set a fair distribution of benefits from the company, should it still exist as our asset. In the event that your sister does not have an active involvement in the company and you do, I will be concerned that her interests are safeguarded. In effect my main concern will be to establish a structure that will avoid serious disagreements within the family after I am gone. I ask you in advance to accept my wishes at that time.

6.   In the event that you wish to confer or disclose personal issues pertaining to your position in the company with another person, Walter and George will be available at those times.

7.   As a member of our management, you will be exposed to confidential company plans and industry secrets. As my son you may be subject to offers from competitive firms or other business offers that would be in competition with us. In joining our company, I ask for your agreement not to accept such offers.

The ideas contained in this letter of agreement have the effect of avoiding some of the potential problems associated with relatives working together in a professional business. The detail and length of this document should not indicate that I am concerned about the success of this arrangement. I believe that it will succeed, and look forward to the pleasure of a manager seeing a young person learning, making decisions, and adding value to the business. As a father, I expect this pleasure to be compounded.

If you agree with the ideas and terms of this letter, I would appreciate your returning a signed copy upon accepting an offer of employment.

Best wishes,

Dad

APPENDIX A

LAWYERS, FAMILIES, AND FEELINGS
Representing the Family Relationship

In 1986, my largest estate-planning client announced that because of age and health, he must step down as CEO of the family business. He asked me to help him teach his children how to work together. He warned me that they didn't get along very well.

My client had strong ideas about what each child ought to want. As often happens, this did not accord with what they really wanted. I was caught in the middle. Who was my client? Was it the business leader alone, or him together with his children, or did I somehow represent the family relationship? If I represented two or more of them, was I an "intermediary" under the Model Code of Professional Responsibility?

In the middle of all this, my client sent over an article that introduced me to family business consulting. Until then I had no idea such a specialty existed. I knew that complex family dynamics were at work and that I didn't understand them. We called in an expert family psychologist who dealt quite skillfully with the family's emotional agenda. Since neither the psychologist nor I had ever run a business, we brought in a third member of the consulting team, a highly successful entrepreneur to function as "ombudsman" for the company to defend its prosperity and its future against any untoward family arrangements.

Eventually, I formed a separate corporation to engage in family business consulting. In our engagement agreements, we undertake to represent the entire family, to help them tap the family resources to provide leadership succession and sensible ownership arrangements. Our goal is "win-win"— that every family member perceive himself or herself as a winner in the process. Our technique is creative aggressive mediation. We help start the difficult conversations, help with communication problems, help set the agenda, guide the discussion, reframe the issues, help the family make decisions, and assign tasks to implement them. As consultants, we don't perform legal services, give tax advice, or do therapy.

Our purpose is to act as catalysts in those areas of family dynamics that have overlapping impact on the health and future of the business. In this role, we may perform some of the functions of "intermediaries." Admittedly, our consulting group was formed because we couldn't find a way to perform these services as lawyers within the ambit of the ethical rules. In the following article,* I examine the lawyer's dilemma in trying to represent families and family businesses.

It is not easy for a lawyer to represent two or more parties in the same transactions. Lawyers' ethical rules require them to disclose to all clients that they may suffer as a result of dual representation, that any client may discharge a lawyer, and that if discharged, a lawyer may not thereafter represent any other parties to the same transaction.

The American College of Trust and Estate Counsel (ACTEC) is currently wrestling with the application of this ethical rule to estate planning for husband and wife. Traditionally, the estate planning lawyer represents the *joint* interests of husband and wife, obtains their joint concurrence to each estate planning step, discloses all information to both, and keeps no communications confidential from either. So common is this approach that few lawyers feel the need to put it in writing in an engagement agreement. In most cases, there is no need to do so.

---

*U.S. Trust Co., "Private Business Advisor," New York, Fall Issue 1991.

Of course, there is no assurance that the interests of husband and wife will remain joint. Suppose the husband later asks the lawyer to change his estate plan, reducing the wife's interest, but also asks the lawyer not to notify the wife of the change. Or suppose the wife calls and tells the lawyer her husband has suffered a stroke that has impaired his judgment. She wants to change her estate plan, but implores the lawyer to not advise her husband of the change for fear of disturbing him.

CONTROVERSIAL PROPOSALS

ACTEC is studying proposals that would permit an estate planning lawyer to represent husbands and wives separately, under a written agreement that would require the lawyer to not disclose communications received from either spouse to the other spouse. As expected, this proposal has caused quite a stir.

Is the estate planning lawyer an "intermediary" between husband and wife if representing them separately? If so, what disclosures are required and which spouse may terminate the professional's services? A more troubling question is whether the estate planning lawyer is also an "intermediary" in undertaking to represent husband and wife jointly.

The dilemma is accentuated in states such as California, where all such engagements are required to be in writing. Must an estate planning lawyer's engagement agreement spell out potential adversary relationships between the spouses? Is estate planning for husbands and wives, whether jointly or separate, to be adversarial in each instance, simply because of the possibility that the marriage may not endure? (Witness the awkwardness of representing an antenuptial agreement to previously unmarried fiancees.) In other words, must the *possibility* of future litigation intrude on the relationship between the estate planning lawyer and the husband and wife clients? Will the trial bar write the relationship?

What often passes for family lawyering involves either implementing the wishes of the dominant family member or persuading the family to adopt the lawyer's sense of fairness under the circumstances. Under the present ethical rules, the only alternative is to inject additional lawyers into the process.

But the introduction of a second lawyer into a family dispute dramatically changes the scenario. The discussion becomes adversarial; family members gather into factions around individual lawyers and begin to talk to each other through their lawyers. From that point on, it is down the slippery slope to taking sides and eventually to litigating family differences in the dark alley of the adversary process.

Too often the family is trapped in lawsuits because family members become enmeshed in a legal system that by implication assumes all human relationships ultimately will fail. The law seeks to assume that human beings who choose to subordinate their individual preferences for the sake of human relationships will ultimately foreswear those relationships. Yet many clients are rediscovering family or family-like relationships that support, nurture, and sustain the family's individual members. The vital, if overworked, word is "relationships."

LAWYERS AND THERAPISTS

The legal world focuses on individuals as basic units in society. Every individual is constitutionally entitled to an advocate to protect himself or herself from all other individuals as adversaries. This assumes a basic life force that is centrifugal, spinning all humans inexorably away from the core of other human beings who reared them, or were reared with them, or are willing to risk reciprocal commitments with them.

Modern psychology takes a different view. The irreducible unit is *not* the individual, but the family. All individuals are creatures of the families in which they were raised, in which they raise their children, and in which eventually they will adore their grandchildren. "Family systems" thinking pervades the psychotherapeutic community and its literature and strongly influences all who counsel families professionally. The rise of marital counseling, family counseling, and crisis intervention, the proliferation of support groups—all testify to a growing awareness of the inextricable relationships between humans.

The ethical dilemma becomes much more complex for the lawyer who represents a family business. Most family business clients do not want to arm for future battles. In one way or another, they want to continue the family business in the context of preserving the family relationship. Most family business members are acutely aware of the hazards and the litigation potential of staying together. In family business consulting, many dominating family members are nevertheless willing to let the mediator help them search for the "greater family good," even though the eventual plan may not perpetuate the founder's strong views, may involve significant compromises, and may incorporate features that no one had even thought of at the time the planning process began.

ACKNOWLEDGING LIMITATIONS

A psychiatrist friend suggests that lawyers and therapists leave client families in the lurch between their respective professional taboos. Most lawyers have difficulty with feelings, their own and their clients'. Clients are expected to take off their emotions before entering their lawyers' temples of reason. Yelling at each other in front of lawyers may well generate legal advice to sell the family business. The lawyer may quickly assume that such unreasonable relatives could not possibly manage a successful business. Distancing the family from its business may manifest the lawyer's distancing from the family's emotional agenda.

The psychiatrist suggests that therapists are just as impractical when it comes to money and property. In the world view of therapists, money and property are merely projections of some internal psychic process, hence unreal. To discuss money and property as though they were real (much less important) is virtually *taboo* among psychotherapists.

It would be tempting to ridicule the therapist fraternity for its aversion to money and property, were most lawyers not equally ridiculous in their aversion to the emotional agenda that client families bring to them. Each profession should confront its own limitations and avoid trying to solve complex problems that lie outside its expertise. Lawyers should at least not make the problem worse.

The flap about representing husbands and wives separately threatens to worsen the situation. Even *joint* representation of husband and wife for estate planning falls short if the estate plan involves (or excludes) other family members. Where family property is involved (whether an ongoing business or not), both family and property should be adequately represented. Many estate planning situations cry out for involvement of the potential recipients in the planning process. Too often the lawyer's office produces estate plans that give children what their parents think they *ought* to want. But without asking the children, how can lawyers and clients be sure the plan will work?

Lawyers must find better ways of representing multiple parties (givers and receivers) in the estate planning transaction. Most families want their relationships preserved and want a single lawyer to help them through the process. As Mark Twain eloquently said, "You never know someone until you share an inheritance with them." But this sharing does not necessarily mean combat. There must be a place for lawyers to help families preserve assets *and* relationships. The two are not necessarily exclusive. Lawyers, families, and feelings must work together.

EPILOGUE

ACTEC is carefully studying the model rules as they impact estate planning for families. The ABA has appointed a special task force for the same purpose. All are concerned that the present ethical rules prevent lawyers from giving their estate planning client families the services they have every reason to demand and deserve.

Even if the ethical rules are relaxed, lawyers who undertake an active role in such "whole-family estate planning" will need to develop new skills and expertise. They will need to understand how the mediation process differs from the adversary process, how to deal with emotional agendas, and how to incorporate family dynamics into the estate plan. Some lawyers are already functioning as mediators out of necessity, or because they have innate skills and talent in family situations. They are risking technical violation of ethical rules for the sake of their family clients. Others are learning how to utilize family business consultants as part of the estate planning team.

I look forward to the day when lawyers are permitted by their ethical rules to function as "whole-family" estate planners and mediators. In such roles, lawyers can justify holding themselves out to the public as both attorneys and counselors.

APPENDIX B

ESTATE PLANNING FOR THE FAMILY BUSINESS OWNER*

Lawyer as Counselor

Historically, the family lawyer has been the prime dispenser of justice to the business family, including dispute resolution. But this traditional role is changing rapidly. There are new threats of malpractice and heightened *malpractice malaise.* When one undertakes to represent a business family, "Who is the *client?*"

Stirred by malpractice malaise, and troubled by ethical rules that contemplate litigation among nonrelated parties, the American College of Trust and Estate Counsel (ACTEC) undertook a thorough review of the Model Rules of Professional Conduct as they apply to the representation of families. ACTEC proposed interpretations of key sections of the Model Rules that would permit trust and estates lawyers to continue their traditional roles.[26]

---

*Reproduced with permission of ALI-ABA. *Remarks by Gerald Le Van at the Annual Meeting of ALI-ABA, Meridien Hotel, San Diego, CA, July 18, 1996.*

179

I was a member of the ACTEC committee that did the work. We published our carefully annotated report thinking that—insofar as family representation is concerned—we had distinguished the ethical constraints on the litigator from the ethical constraints on the trusts and estates lawyer. Otherwise put, we had separated the ethical rules of battle from the ethical rules of cooperation and collaboration.

ACTEC's president invited Professor Geoffrey Hazard of Yale Law School, and reporter on the American Law Institute's project on *The Law of Lawyering*, to lecture at our annual meeting and to evaluate the ACTEC commentaries on the Model Rules. Although I did not attend, I'm told that Professor Hazard rejected ACTEC's proposed distinctions out of hand, insisting that the Model Rules apply unswervingly to every situation in which a lawyer undertakes to represent two or more clients, whether there is litigation or not, whether they are family or not.

Skills Deficit: Mediation, Facilitation, Psychology

I learned (and taught) very little in law school about family dynamics, family systems, conflict resolution, or family psychology. Ten years ago, my two largest estate-planning clients were successful and contentious family businesses. I tried to mediate. I tried to preside over family meetings. I tried to use what insights I had gained from my own family of origin and my nuclear family to cope with my clients' family conflicts. I was in over my head. And today, after ten intensive years of family business consulting, I would *still* be over my head if I tried to help business families as their lawyer all alone. Perhaps I wouldn't make as many blunders, but by myself, I couldn't possibly give them all of what they need.

Loss of the Client: Fallout from Family Conflict

Though I can't prove it statistically, I am anecdotally persuaded that business families who get their conflicts resolved without too much trauma tend to retain their outside advisors, including their lawyers. Deserve it or not, the lawyer gets part of the *credit* for their safe navigation. Likewise, I am anecdotally persuaded that business families who go through wrenching trauma, conflict, and misery tend to replace their outside advisors, including their lawyers. Deserve it or not, we get the *blame* for their misery.

If my anecdotal wisdom is sound, you have a *bottom line* interest in minimizing their trauma as business families go through their inevitable transitions, inevitable *changes* in their lives together.

The "Business Family" in Broad Perspective

Notice my use of the words "business family" instead of the term "family business." We prefer to think and talk about "business families." The word "family" as the noun focuses primary attention where it belongs—on the family rather than the business. "Family business" almost always connotes an operating company and its three most common problems:

1. whether to keep or sell

2. if kept, then management succession, and

3. if kept, how to reconcile inside and outside shareholders.

"Business families" may own or control operating companies, but those companies may be a minor part of family wealth. Some of the families you and I represent are not at all involved in operating companies, but are very much "business families" bound together by all kinds of common interests in family-generated wealth.

Although some families insist that their businesses or fortunes are managed solely according to business values bereft of family influence, I seldom believe it. Family dynamics are just too pervasive, too emotionally powerful, too omnipresent to be excluded from the business equation. More often than not, family dynamics so dominate the business family that their business judgment becomes skewed, even distorted.

The goal of family business consultants is to help business

families deal with those family dynamics in the mutual interest of the business and the family, with the result that *the family exercises its best informed collective judgment.* When this is done, the family has done the best it can do. The family's best collective judgment usually suffices.

Family Litigation

The last ten years has provided me with a graphic refresher course on the destructive power of family litigation, even the threat of family litigation. Litigation is the brooding omnipresence that hovers over every potentially contentious business family. Your chief allies in litigation avoidance are family members themselves. They don't want litigators, or litigation. They want to learn to cooperate, to collaborate, to co-exist; or, i.e. at least, to *manage* their differences. They don't want independence so much as a workable *interdependence.*

Now and then it's necessary to work out a *civil disengagement* between family members or family branches; to divide companies, reorganize assets, structure *apartness* unhappily, thereby dashing the dreams of the founder that somehow all will work together and be happy together. But the gross *in*civility of family litigation is certainly *not* the way to accomplish healthy civil disengagement .

The 1980s Model

Consulting to business families is very new. Its acknowledged founder is Leon Danco of Cleveland, who grew to prominence in the 1980s. Other pioneers in counseling business families came from organizational development (OD) and from clinical psychology. By training and disposition, good ODs are sensitive both to business necessities and to emotional agendas. Their role is not so "prescriptive" as it is collaborative—to be a member of a team that solves an organizational problem. Their OD penchant is that organization and structure are the cause and cure of most business problems. Hence their bent to organizational solutions for the family such as outside boards of directors, mission or vision statements, codes of conduct for family members, and other devices that would mold the family into a manageable, rational, business organization which, unfortunately, *it isn't and can't become.* (I'm not disparaging any of those organizational devices. We use each of them.)

Clinical psychologists and family therapists came to family business both from their training in family systems and their clinical experience with the emotional wreckage in some business families. We are much in their debt for the application of family systems psychology to business families—in my view, their greatest contribution. I would not assign a family therapist to work alone with a business family. Their training and discipline creates in most of them a professional *aversion* to money and property—*a taboo* that invites neglect of the very important business issues.

However, let me hastily add that I would not undertake to counsel *any* business family without a family therapist on the team. Their expertise is indispensable as *collaborative consultants.* (They do not do therapy with the family. Therapy is an individual matter.) You may be thinking that your hard-nosed clients wouldn't talk to a psychologist, and they would question your wisdom in recommending a team that includes one. Think again. I ask you to question your own bias. From experience in litigation, you may think of psychologists as "whores"—as expert witnesses who say their peace and are then hurried out of the deposition or courtroom. It's very likely that your client families have *already seen* psychologists for individual, marital, or other counseling. They don't share your disinclination to "touchy-feely," your tendency to think of psychologists as "whores."

THE FAMILY BUSINESS ENVIRONMENT

Let me describe some of the messages and organizations that are out there for business families today.

The Family Firm Institute

There are no licensing requirements for family business consultants, no required curriculum, no professional examinations, no disciplinary rules. In fact, there is no formal consensus about what family business consultants should do or what client families are entitled to expect. Though strongly affected by their disciplines of origin, family business consultants usually don't do it as a part of their professional practice.

Family business consultants are very loosely organized into the Family Firm Institute (FFI), formed in the 1980s. By comparison to our state bar associations, FFI is struggling, at times chaotic, but improving. Most leading family business consultants belong to FFI and participate to some extent. FFI provides a gathering point for all of the disciplines that are fascinated and frustrated by business families. Until recently, few lawyers belonged to FFI, and those few were "recovering lawyers" like myself.

The Media

Some claim the media has a liberal bias. Some say it's a conservative bias. I agree with those who maintain that the media has a palpably *negative* bias. Bad news sells; good news bores. This negative bias permeates family business news in most of the leading publications. This negative news pounding reinforces apprehensions of doom that already abound in business families.

On the other hand, *Nations' Business, Family Business Journal, Family Business Magazine,* and sometimes *Inc.* carry the positive stories about business families who have their acts together. Unfortunately, some of the positive stories turn out to be unreliable public relations constructs.

The Family Business Forums

Begun in Atlanta, these organized self-help groups are spreading. Members are a limited number of local business families. Most forums are sponsored by a local university business school, by local law firms, national or regional accounting firms, and life insurance companies or agents; all of these sponsors interested in marketing to business families.

The forums do a good job of consciousness-raising. It's important for business families to realize they are *not alone* in their tensions and conflicts, and the forums provide consolation and positive reinforcement. My understanding is that the typical business family drops out of a forum during the second year of membership, after most of the primary family business topics have been addressed.

Trade Associations

Certain industries and market segments have heavy business family involvement. These may include new car dealers, funeral directors, general contractors, and, of course, farming and ranching. The Young Presidents Organization draws heavily from business families. Some franchisors have a bottom-line interest in the continued *success* of their family-owned franchises. Other franchisors have a bottom-line interest in their *failure* and are poised to gobble up conflicted family franchises when the family throws in the towel.

Lawyer Response

Law firms are beginning to respond to their business family clients in new ways. A systematic review of client lists may reveal that business families are a substantial source of your firm income. Further checking may show that these clients have grown substantially since your firm last rendered significant services, and are now prime prospects for more sophisticated representation.

In larger firms, there may be a serious lack of coordination between the tax section, corporate section, and the trusts and estates group. Some firms have formed interdepartmental "family business groups" to focus on services to business families.

The Tax Section and Probate and Property Section of the American Bar Association seem more tuned in to business families. ALI-ABA sponsors an annual seminar on estate planning for the family business owner. Some lawyers belonging to the Family Firm Institute have formed a promising new group, Attorneys for Family Held Enterprise.

Academia

Some of the graduate business schools have discovered family business. Once ignored in the curriculum, family business courses and research projects are springing up around the country. There is a good bit of academic influence in the Family Firm Institute and in its *Family Business Review*.

As a former law professor, I'm aware of the hazards of academics as consultants. One hazard is the passionate injection of academic theory without a working appreciation of business reality. Another hazard is the client's excessive and unrealistic deference to academic credentials, particularly among business families that have limited contact with higher education. With some exceptions, I'm dubious about academics who moonlight as family business consultants. Nevertheless, for the serious scholar learning and teaching about the phenomenology of family business is a huge and fascinating undertaking.

CPA Response

I have long envied the relationship between the outside CPA and his or her business family client. They meet regularly and talk about money. Typically, the CPA prepares the company tax return and the individual returns of family members, dispensing financial advice along the way, taking on the role of a fiscal father (or mother) confessor.

CPAs get an earful of family conflicts usually during tax season, when they are grasping for details and can't give their full attention to the family's troubles. Some of the big-six firms have taken quite a public position as counselors to family business. At least one regional firm offers comprehensive consulting services to business families that includes the psychological dimension. AICPA (American Institute of Certified Public

Accountants) and some of the regional alliances of accounting firms are also showing interest. Recently, I met with the leadership of one of these alliances that is searching for the appropriate role of the outside accountant with the business family. They acknowledged that a client's plea for advice about family business tensions can be a Catch-22. The accountant seems forced either to refuse advice (and thereby appear disinterested) or to "wing it" with advice that may not be informed or appropriate. Most admitted they "wing it" rather than risk appearing disinterested.

Family Therapy Response
With the advent of managed care, expect a large number of clinical psychologists to leave active practice and to look for other work. As one put it, "I can't abide some clerk dictating how often I can see a patient who is potentially suicidal!" These exiting psychologists will find family business consulting attractive, but will carry with them their built-in taboos against money and property. On the brighter side, they will constitute an attractive pool of talent for multidisciplinary consulting teams.

Insurance Industry
Massachusetts Mutual has published an interesting survey of family businesses that is well worth reading. The company has also produced a good videotape that introduces family business issues. The Million Dollar Roundtable is scheduling more sessions on family business, and more family business articles are appearing in insurance magazines.

Although I see huge largely untapped potential for insurance sales to business families, and strong relationships between business families and their insurance agents, I don't yet see the companies or their agents capitalizing on these opportunities. For example, preoccupation with second-to-die insurance to pay estate taxes overlooks the need to fund buyouts on the death of the business leader, usually the first-to-die.

Financial Community Response

Banks and investment bankers have made a checkered response to business families. Some money center banks and the super regionals offer investment banking services to business families whose size doesn't meet the usual $100 million minimum that interests Wall Street. Money center banks and super regionals have made special appeals to their middle market customers with gross revenues ranging from approximately $5 million to $200 million, replete with business families.

However, there is considerable complaint that most money centers and super regionals are no longer interested in the middle market. Second and third tier banks are trying to take up the slack by courting these middle market family businesses.

The High Net-Worth Family

Contemplating the fabled "$10 trillion wealth transfer," the very rich business family is receiving a great deal of attention. "Raising rich kids" has spawned a new consultant cottage industry.

Once a vehicle of the super rich, family offices are proliferating to provide cradle-to-grave services to members of wealthy families from household management, to travel services, to surrogate parenting, to trust administration. (Some family companies already provide these services in-house on a less formal basis.)

Very upscale, private banking is becoming an art form. More families are chartering their own private trust companies— disillusioned by the services offered by corporate trustees, or fearful that individual trustees will become embroiled in family fiduciary litigation.

Too many of these upscale families are struggling to conform family dynamics to rigid estate plans created two or three generations ago:

- estate plans that may continue for several more generations;

- estate plans that are badly out of joint with the family system;

- estate plans that have created serious relationship problems for their beneficiaries.

I worry that we overuse QTIP (Qualified Terminable Interest Trust) planning today, creating matriarchies that will spawn similar problems down the line.

International Family Business Organizations and Efforts
In Western Europe, South America, and in the Pacific Rim, family ownership of very large businesses is quite common. Public ownership of large companies is much less common, where securities exchanges are less developed. Though cultural norms may vary, family dynamics are powerfully at work in these giant foreign companies.

PART II.   EVOLUTION OF FAMILY BUSINESS CONSULTING

Consultants as *Facilitators*
There is a major difference between advisors, organizational consultants, and process consultants. Most family business consultants operate as process consultants. Their premise is that business families must ask and answer certain critical questions about their future for themselves. Answers that harness the best collective business judgment of the family are usually good enough.

The function of the process consultant is to see that these questions are asked, properly discussed, answered, and the answers implemented. "Process consulting" is a kind of Socratic prompting that stimulates the family to discover its own issues, reach its own conclusions, and, in the course of things, develop its own process for addressing future concerns.

The process consultant is not a guru, advisor, or opinion giver. The process consultants are merely a facilitators, catalysts. They do not supplant the family's traditional advisors, whose function is to give advice. They are close collaborators with the family lawyers. Their goal is to understand and mobilize the dynamics in the business family so that the business planning and the estate planning and the family system *fit together*. In my opinion, the best family business consultants are process consultants.

In this era of alternate dispute resolution, the mediation process may be described as *assisted settlement negotiations*. In many respects, a good mediator is a "process consultant" in the context of the legal process. Properly done, family business consulting may be accurately described as *assisted decision-making* with business families.

Later Generation Transitions

A few GI generation entrepreneurs are still working into their seventies. Apart from them, the GI generation model of the family business is dated. Lots of GI generation businesses are already in second-generation ownership and management. The preponderance of founding entrepreneurs these days belong to my generation, the silent generation. Businesses founded before World War II may be in their third or even fourth generation of family ownership.

As ownership passes down generations, there are more relatives who are less closely related. They are tied together mostly by their business and financial interests. They may have inherited wealth in the form of stock in businesses they did not create, businesses they don't understand, businesses to which they have contributed neither time nor talent. Too often theirs is an unfortunate mixture of investor mentality and "entitlement" mentality. Their attitude and manner reminds us of royalty.

As they perceive it, birthright entitles them to maintain the family standard of living off of the company, and it's up to the management to make that happen—business conditions notwithstanding. (All of us have observed this "royalty entitlement" attitude among trust beneficiaries.) Tensions between inside and outside shareholders in a business family can be fierce. We call this phenomenon "The Parasites vs. The Plunderers." In older generation companies, shareholding may be so widespread that no person or family line has voting control. Voting control may be exercised by trustees who have the impossible task of reconciling Parasites and Plunderers.

Entrepreneurial Style Accedes to MBA Style

America has long been the hotbed and haven of entrepreneuring. The rugged, driven, charismatic, risk-taking, intuitive (sometimes chaotic), highly successful entrepreneur has become a folk hero. Although the "GI entrepreneurial style" is pursued by their juniors, the size, complexity, and velocity of modern business is challenging entrepreneurial style. Even during first-generation ownership, we see larger family businesses forced to adopt the more traditional MBA management approach. Successor management in later generations is almost always much closer to business school managerial model. Lost to the business is the force of strong leadership the entrepreneur once provided.

While we estate planners are preoccupied with successor ownership, the family is likely to be preoccupied with successor *management* issues and the approaching *void of leadership* both in the business and perhaps also in the family. There's always a possibility that we and the family aren't on the same page with our primary concerns.

For us lawyers, the aging entrepreneur can be at once our most prized and our most puzzling client. As a key employee described his wildly successful entrepreneurial boss to me: "It's uncanny how often Fred is right—for the wrong reasons!"

Entrepreneurial style doesn't work well inside families, just as lawyering style doesn't work well inside families. Do you ever find yourself cross-examining a four-year-old, or a fourteen-year-old who knows you are a *dork*? Families don't want to be *led* or *lawyered*; families want to be loved and nurtured. Try removing your professional mask of invulnerability and hang it outside the door before you walk in your house. Show the inhabitants your vulnerable side, your needy side. They will likely do the same. This is what families are about.

Family Dynamics Focus

Traditionally, lawyers have been called upon to do estate plans that implement the business leader's wishes as to the future of the family business. Traditionally, estate planning was done in secret and the successors were kept in the dark until the will was read. Increasingly, however, business leaders understand how the future of the family business impacts the whole family. Increasingly, business families understand the importance of *intergenerational* estate planning that involves wide-ranging *dialogue* between the givers and the receivers, the parasites and the plunderers; between those successor managers who are asked to invest their *lives* in the business and successor owners who are asked to leave their inheritance at the risk of the business.

There needs to be a safe forum where every person who has or may acquire a stake in the family business may speak openly and candidly. Some families do this dialogue with grace. Other families require facilitators to prompt them and coach them toward *assisted decision-making.* I'm not suggesting that these family meetings become Athenian democracies that dictate the estate plan by majority vote. I do suggest that by giving each potential stakeholder a voice and a dignified audience, he or she is much more likely to *buy into the plan.* Whether or not a family member gets his or her way, the process of participation in intergenerational estate planning for the family business can create a genuine *win-win* atmosphere in which a family member perceives he or she has been treated *fairly,* after a *fair hearing* and a *fair* exchange of views. This atmosphere of *fairness* can make a profound difference in how the estate plan is received. (Issues between older and younger generations usually involve power and control. Issues between members of same generation involve *fairness.*)

You may have the skills to plan and conduct such meetings for your business family clients. If you don't have those skills, you may want to cultivate them. *Until* you have those skills, you risk at best, disappointing your client business family; at worst, hurting them.

Multidisciplinary Team Consulting

The 1980s consulting model stressed indispensability of a single, wizened, business consultant who gave advice. The sheer size and complexity of larger business families makes it impossible for one person both to facilitate and observe. Even in smaller business families, the sheer *intensity* of the presenting problem may require multiple consultants from different disciplines.[27]

The 1980s consulting model didn't stress any particular qualifying discipline. According to that model, the consultant must have had an understanding of business, an ability to identify with the founder, and possess some anecdotal wisdom. Though early on the organizational development experts and the family therapists struggled for dominance, I doubt that *any* of the traditional helping professions will corner the market. Nor do I foresee the emergence of a new specialized profession of family business consulting. Unfortunately, many will continue in their individual professions (including lawyers) myopically struggling to meet the manifold needs of business families by plying their traditional training and skills—and *failing to meet the family's needs*. Fortunately, I also think we will see a great expansion of team consulting, where I believe the responsible future lies.

Conforming the Estate Plan to Family Dynamics

This leading edge of multidisciplinary team consulting to business families will impact estate planning. The time is coming, if it isn't already here, when business families will expect their estate plans to conform to family dynamics. Business families will demand *congruence* between their family systems and their wealth transfers.

To respond, estate planners must become more informed and sensitive to family dynamics. And because most estate planners will *never* have the skills or inclination to assess family dynamics, they must come to rely on others to do that important work.

Where a business family is involved, the traditional estate planning team will expand—is expanding—to include family business consultants whose responsibility it will be to:

- assess the family system

- grasp and monitor family dynamics

- facilitate family communications

- inform and update the estate planners about family issues that bear on the planning process

- generally assist family and advisors to see that wealth planning accords with family dynamics

PART III.   SOME LESSONS WE HAVE LEARNED

1.   *The resources for solutions to the most important issues lie* **within the family.** There are no quick, cheap, simple fixes, no "magic bullets." The family must ask themselves the critical questions, and find their own answers through an acceptable *process* for dialogue, discussion, deliberation, and decision.

2.   *"Win-win" is the only acceptable solution to family differences.* "Win-*lose*" almost always becomes "*lose-lose.*" "Win-win" is not compromise. In compromise situations, one plus one is less than two. In "win-win" situations, one plus one is greater than two.

3.   *Some advisor must be ombudsman for the* **entire family.** If legal ethics don't permit representation of the entire family, some other advisor must take the role. The consultant's client is the *family relationship,* although the family company usually pays the bills.

4.   *"Communication" is a threshold problem in most conflicted families.* Families we see are "stuck" and cannot talk productively about the very issues that need dialogue. They must

find their way out of a communications blackout. Improving communications involves not only *what* they discuss, but *how* they talk to each other. Both the words and the *music* are important. Bad communications can co-exist in good families. Bad communications are usually symptomatic of more fundamental issues. However, bad communications are rarely if ever the *cause* of their conflict.

5. *It is indispensable to understand the family as a system.* Understanding the system begins with interviewing them in depth together and separately. Individual confidential interviews with each family member are *absolutely indispensable* to an understanding of the family system. This includes individual interviews with spouses, kept confidential from the other spouse. Ordinarily individual interviews should *precede* meetings of the family as a whole. A premature family meeting can do harm. Family members may need coaching about the techniques of successful meetings before a family meeting can be productive.

6. *Sequence.* Separating relationship issues from business issues is much more difficult if important business decisions demand immediate attention—e.g., if the business leader has just died unexpectedly. Where the situation permits, the families' advisors are usually understanding and are willing to hold off planning decisions until the family has improved its communications.

7. *Relationships with the family's outside advisors.* Some outside advisors prefer to stay very close to the consulting process. They may attend family meetings and receive frequent briefings on the family's progress. Other advisors prefer to maintain distance from the process at least while the emotional and relationship issues are being addressed. They are concerned with being "dumped on" (somehow blamed) by the family for its problems. "Wake me when it's over," they tell us.

8. *Having team members with business expertise maintains relevance.* Having them on the team *from the outset* keeps us from losing sight of business issues. Their interaction with family

therapy team members helps identify the business options that are most likely to fit the family system. Their combination of business skills and expertise is much more likely to provide outside advisors with input that produces workable "win-win" situations.

9.   *Sometimes the best solution is a "civil disengagement."* In the interest of the family as a whole, it may be best that business relationships are reduced or dissolved, and that personal relationships be more distant, less intense, less likely to provoke conflict. Properly done, these civil disengagements can be win-win. Because of the complexity of many family business structures, business disengagements can be monumentally difficult.

10.   *Sometimes there is a positive "delayed reaction."* Now and then a client family will discontinue our services before the consultants think they have reached a good solution. Months or even years later the family will finish the process on its own.

DOLLARS AND CHANGE

Most of the important transactions you handle for business families involve fundamental changes in the family system:

- births, deaths, marriages, divorces

- change in business leaders, change in business owners, sale of the business

You watch the dollars, while the family tries to cope with the change. Dollars and change. In the past, we estate planners have focused on the dollars and largely ignored the change. Listen to your competitors' message to your business family clients:

"We understand the changes that confront you; let us watch your dollars!"

Change is threatening to families. In many respects, the function of family life is to *resist* change. But change is inevitable. The current business leader must eventually step down. The business will either be sold, or managed by someone else. Sons and daughters will either manage the company, or it will be managed by a nonrelative. Perhaps *"transition"* is a less threatening word, and we often use the word "transition" instead of the word "change." To business families "change" may connote something strange, foreign, invasive, malignant, something inconsistent, even hostile to family values and the family's ways of doing things.

The necessary changes or rearrangements don't necessarily subvert family values or family solidarity. Most constructive change merely involves tapping unused family resources, organizing these resources, restructuring, reforming, restarting. *Benign rearrangements,* not hostile change. Change from within, not change from without. Most families will accept benign rearrangements.

Your estate planning should propose benign rearrangements that fit the family.

NOTES

1. Pottker, Jan. *Born to Power: Heirs to America's Leading Business.* New York: Barron's Educational Series, 1992, p. 233.

2. Ibid., p. 218.

3. Ibid., p. 170.

4. Ibid., p. 206.

5. Ibid., p. 219.

6. Dumas, Collette. "Understanding of Father-Daughter and Father-Son Dyads in Family-Owned Businesses." *Family Business Review* 2, I (Spring 1989).

7. Pottker, *Born to Power*, p. 200.

8. Ibid., p. 228.

9. Ibid., p. 239.

10. Ibid., p. 294.

11. Ibid., p. 306.

12. Ibid., p. 259.

13. Ibid., p. 225.

14. Kenney, Charles. *Riding the Runaway Horse: The Rise and Decline of Wang Laboratories.* Boston: Little Brown, 1992.

15. Pottker, *Born to Power*, p. 106.

16. Powell, Colin. *My American* Journey (New York: Random House, 1995), p. 166.

17. Pottker, *Born to Power*, p. 22.

18. Ibid., p. 289.

19. Ibid., p. 186.

20. Ibid., p. 199.

21. Ibid., p. 393.

22. Ibid., p. 64.

23. Ibid., p. 249.

24. Ibid., p. 313.

25. Ibid., p. 444.

26. Ibid., p. 366.

27. See *ACTEC Commentaries on Model Rules of Professional Conduct, October 1993.* See especially, MRPC 1.4 (communication), 1.6 (confidentiality), 1.7 (conflict of interest), 2.2 (lawyer as intermediary).

28. See Le Van, "Rapproachment between Family Wealth Management and Family Systems," Keynote Address, Family Firm Institute, October 1995 (hereafter Le Van FFI Keynote) Proceedings of Family Firm Institute—audio taped.

SUGGESTED READING

BOOKS

Business Tactics

Aronoff, Craig, and John Ward, eds. *Family Business Sourcebook*. Detroit: Omnigraphics, 1990.

———. *Family Business Succession: the Final Test of Greatness*. Marietta: Business Owner Resources, 1996.

Bork, David, et al., eds. *Working With Family Businesses: A Guide for Professionals*. San Francisco: Jossey-Bass, 1995.

Bucholz, Barbara B., and Margaret Crane. *Corporate Bloodlines: The Future of the Family Firm* New York: Carol Publishing, 1989.

Cohn, Mike. *Passing the Torch: Succession, Retirement, and Estate Planning in Family Owned Businesses*. New York: McGraw-Hill, 1992.

Dyer, W.G., Jr. *Cultural Changes in Family Firms: Anticipating and Managing Business and Family Transitions*. San Francisco: Jossey-Bass, 1986.

Gersick, Kelin E., Johna A. Davis, Marion McCollum Hampton, and Ivan Lansberg. *Generation to Generation: Life Cycles of the Family Business*. Boston: Harvard Business School Press, 1996.

Henning, Mike. *Your Final Test for Success*. Effingham, IL: Henning Family Business Center, 1992.

Jaffe, Dennis T. *Working With the Ones You Love: Conflict Resolution and Problem Solving Strategies for a Successful Family Business*. Berkeley, CA: Conari Press, 1990.

Jonovic, Donald J. *The Ultimate Legacy: How Owners of Family and Closely Held Businesses Can Achieve Their Real Purpose*. Cleveland, OH: Jamieson, 1997.

Kleberg, Sally S. *The Stewardship of Private Wealth: Managing Personal and Family Financial Assets*. New York: McGraw-Hill, New York, 1997.

Nelton, Sharon. *How Entrepreneurial Couples Are Changing the Rules of Business and Marriage*. New York: Wiley, 1986.

Poza, Ernesto. *Smart Growth: Critical Choices for Business Continuity and Prosperity*. San Francisco: Jossey-Bass, 1989.

Rosenblatt, Paul F., Leni De Mik, Roxanne Marie Anderson, Patrica A. Johnson. *The Family in Business*. San Francisco: Jossey-Bass, 1985.

Sulloway, Frank J. *Born to Rebel: Birth Order, Family Dynamics, and Creative Lives*. Pantheon Books, 1996.

Ward, John. *Keeping the Family Business Healthy: How to Plan for Continuing Growth, Profitability, and Family Leadership*. San Francisco: Jossey-Bass, 1987.

Ward, John L. *Creating Effective Boards*. San Francisco: Jossey-Bass, 1991.

Family Business Histories

Broehl, Wayne G., Jr. *Cargill: Trading the Word's Grain*. Hanover, NH: University Press of New England, 1992.

Collier, P., and D. Horowitz. *The Fords: An American Epic*. New York: Summit, 1987.

Kenney, Charles C., *Riding the Runaway Horse: the Rise and Decline of Wang Laboratories*. Boston: Little Brown, 1992.

O'Brien, Robert. *Marriott: The J. Willard Marriott Story*. Salt Lake City, UT: Deseret Book Co., 1979.

Spector, Robert, and Patrick D. McCarthy. *The Nordstrom Way: The Inside Story of America's #1 Customer Service Company*. New York: Wiley, 1995.

Articles

Lorsch, Jay W. "Empowering the Board," *Harvard Business Review* (January–February 1995).

"Redraw the Line Between the Board and the CEO," *Harvard Business Review* (March–April, 1995).

MAGAZINES

Family Business, PO Box 41966, Philadelphia, PA 19101. Telephone: 215-790-7000.

Family Business, The Stoy Centre for Family Business, 8 Baker Street, London W1M 1DA. Telephone: 0171 486 5888.

Family Business Review, 12 Harris Street, Brookline, MA 02146. Telephone: 617-738- 1591.

Nation's Business, 1615 H Street, NW, Washington, DC 20062-2000. Telephone: 202-463-5650.

ORGANIZATIONS

Attorneys for Family Held Enterprise,77 Prospect Avenue, Box 4A, Hackensack, NJ, 07601. Telephone: 201-488-9323. Attorneys for Family Held Enterprise is a professional, non-profit organization dedicated to educating attorneys in the skills needed to successfully represent family businesses.

Family Business Education Forums and Centers. Universities throughout the United States and other countries offer programs to promote effective family business management, as well as a forum for business families and their advisors to obtain and exchange information both from a family perspective and a business perspective. The Family Firm Institute has a listing of forums and centers that are members of their organization, or check with your state or country's universities.

Family Firm Institute Inc., 12 Harris Street, Brookline, MA 02146. Telephone 617-738-1591. The Family Firm Institute is an international, professional organization dedicated to assisting family firms by increasing the interdisciplinary skills and knowledge of family business advisors, educators, researchers, and consultants.

WEBSITES

Family Firm Institute: http://ffi.org Provides information, networking, and professional development for practitioners serving family business.

NetMarque Family Business Net Center: http://nmq.com/FamBizNC

An online, business information resource serving owners and executives of small and emerging companies and family-held firms.

The most comprehensive and helpful website for business families is Family Business Roundtable's at fbrinc.com. It carries reviews of family business publications, latest news affecting business families, case studies, even job-posting.

Index

stock (*cont.*)
strategic planning, xviii
stuck families, xiii, xviii, 194–195
succession
  in family businesses, 81–93, 117, 191
  guidelines for, 87
Sun City [computer game], xvii
surrogates, for wealthy children, 65, 66, 67, 188
suspicion, in inheritors, 61–62
sweat equity
  compensation for, 154
  generated by business families, 59

tagalong clause, role in family buyouts, 114–115
tax
  on family business estate, 113
  role in family business sale, 52
teenagers, in business families, xviii
termination, of family business members, 155
Thomas, Dave, 61
"touchy feely" issues, in stuck families, xviii
tough love, use for financial distress, 136
trade associations, for family businesses, 185
transition, meaning to business families, 198
triangulation, among managers, daughters, and mothers, 31
trust companies, for high net-worth family, 188
trusts, xviii
Twain, Mark, 176

underpraise, of family business successor, 91
"Understanding Father-Daughter and Father-Son Dyads in Family-Owned Businesses (Dumas), 29–30
United Way, family business's contributions to, 146

unwritten rules, in family businesses, 89, 92–93

videotape, of family business, 6

"walk through", of family business sale, 50–52, 53
Wal-Mart Stores, Inc., 54, 149
Walton, S. Robson, 54
Walton, Sam, 149
Wang, An, 5, 76–77, 78, 79–80, 91
Wang, Courtney, 77, 80
Wang, Fred, as president of Wang Laboratories, 77, 80, 91
Wang Laboratories, rise and fall of, 76–80, 91
Wang Word Processing System, 77, 78
wealth
  constructive attitudes about, 68
  fear of loss of, 65
websites, for family business information, 203
Wendy's International, Inc., 61
Western Europe, business families in, xi, 189
wills, xviii
"win-win" goal, of family business members, 172, 194
women, problems with wealth of, 64
work ethic, of JacMar Corporation, 119
work relationships, in family businesses, 118
work responsibilities, of family business members, 54
work styles, gender based, 30

Yale Law School, 180
younger members, of business families, xviii, 126
youngest children
  as America's founders, 18
  marriage of, 17
  qualities of, 16
Young Presidents Organization, family business leaders in, 185